The SELLING of Canada

A

For my mother and father,
who set me on course

The Selling of Canada,
© 1983 by Altitude Publishing Ltd.,
Box 490, Banff, Alberta, Canada
T0L 0C0

All Rights Reserved

Text: *The Selling of Canada*
© 1983 E.J. Hart

ISBN: 0-919381-09-X

The SELLING of Canada

The CPR and the Beginnings of Canadian Tourism

E. J. Hart

Published by
Altitude Publishing Ltd.
Banff, Canada

Acknowledgements

As is usual in a work of this type, the author owes a debt of gratitude to numerous people for their assistance in making it possible.

First and foremost, I would like to express my thanks to Margery Hadley for her valuable assistance in researching Van Horne's papers. In a typical act of selflessness, she made notations on references in the papers that would be useful to my subject while researching her Master's topic on western Canadian landscape photographers. Without her kindness this book would not have been possible.

Secondly, to Omer Lavallée, CPR Corporate Archivist, and his staff, particularly Cecil Halsey, for their assistance in providing valuable research material and illustrations. Omer's assistance went well beyond the bounds of normal professional service to the kindness of reading the manuscript for historical accuracy. Cecil and other staff members delved deeply into the CPR's treasure trove of advertising material to find many items that were indispensable for the written and visual content of this book.

As usual, other colleagues in the archival profession were helpful above and beyond the call of duty. In this regard I would like to especially acknowledge Bill McKee, Georgeen Klassen and the staff at the Glenbow Archives, Barry Hyman and Betty Blight at the Manitoba Provincial Archives, Stanley Triggs at the Notman Archives, Joan Schwartz at the Public Archives of Canada, Les McCann at the Vancouver Maritime Museum, the staff at the Provincial Archives of Alberta, Sue Baptie at the City of Vancouver Archives and John Bovey at the Provincial Archives of British Columbia.

I also thank Jacqueline Hunter of The National Gallery in Ottawa who suggested historical paintings which added greatly to this volume, and Dr. Donald Grace of Calgary who very kindly lent me the use of his collection.

I would also like to pay tribute to the work of two fine editors, Jane and Martin Lynch, who are largely responsible for making this manuscript readable. And finally, to Carole Harmon and Stephen Hutchings of Altitude Publishing for having enough faith in the project to become personally involved in its creation and support its publication.

Banff, Alberta, May, 1983

Contents

Westbound CPR steam locomotive on the first Mountain Creek Bridge.
O. B. Buell photograph

"Mountain Scene," Lucius O'Brien, 1886, watercolour, 35.6 x 54.6 cm.

Introduction

The holiday or vacation is a recent phenomenon, a function of the upper and middle classes first exercised in the middle of the nineteenth century. Initially the desire to escape the city and the workplace for the health-giving country air took the form of local excursions and later, as transportation services in the form of railroads and steamships began to improve, they were extended to include seaside and mountain resorts. The business of tourism that resulted from this movement was by the last decades of the century a well-developed and often lucrative enterprise.

Into this rapidly developing world of tourism the Canadian Pacific Railway was born. In 1870 the Canadian government found it prudent to promise the construction of a transcontinental railway in return for British Columbia's agreement to enter Confederation. The construction was fraught with great difficulties, economic, political and physical, but through the great tenacity of its financial backers, the CPR Syndicate, the foresight of its political standardbearer, the Conservative government of John A. Macdonald, and the genius of its general manager, William Cornelius Van Horne, the work was completed in 1885. But it was completed at such a cost that the company immediately began examining every possible avenue of making money to reduce its enormous debt load and to pay its heavy operating costs. Thus Van Horne responded to the CPR's particularly expensive — and beautiful — mountain section with a money-making proposition: "If we can't export the scenery, we'll import the tourists." From this philosophy of "capitalizing the scenery" the CPR developed its overwhelming presence in Canadian tourism. By the 1920s, its tourist operations embraced Canada from coast to coast and spanned the world. For several decades its tourist advertising delineated the view of Canada, both at home and around the world. Its view of Canada as a place of scenic wonders and cultural diversity prevails even to this day.

This book will examine the CPR's tourist operations, its well-orchestrated tourist advertising campaigns, its tourist facilities, and the tourists themselves, from the beginning of transcontinental service in 1886 to the coming of the automobile and the flowering of the Canadian Pacific's steamship services in the 1920s. The focus is on the mountain region of the Canadian west, the crowning glory of the railway's tourist program. The leading characters are Van Horne, George Ham and John Murray Gibbon, who, in their careers with the CPR, were major influences on Canadian tourism and Canadian culture.

The author recognizes that the tourist phenomenon was a small part of overall CPR operations, unworthy of a separate bookkeeping entry. Passenger rail service in its totality during the four decades after the completion of the line took a back seat to freight traffic as is evidenced by an examination of earnings. In 1886 freight earnings were $6,112,380 and by 1920 had grown to $145,303,400. Over the same period passenger earnings grew from $2,768,840 to $49,125,740. Furthermore, the percentage of tourist-generated earnings in these totals was relatively small; during this period of massive immigration to the Canadian west and rapid branch-line construction it was the immigrant and local passenger that produced much of them. Somewhat similar figures could be quoted for CPR steamship operations, which also included a tourist element. Perhaps only in hotels did the tourist play a major role in profit-making.

But the balance sheet is a poor measure of the importance and significance of CPR tourism. Even if it did not turn out to be as lucrative as some had hoped, it was nonetheless exceedingly valuable to the company and the country. Through the company's efforts Canada was for the first time "sold" to the rest of the world, as a place for settlement in its immigration campaigns, and as a travel destination in its tourist promotions. A positive world view of Canada was the result. This, in turn, undoubtedly influenced such factors as immigration, trade and international political relations. Equally, if not more importantly, it also enabled Canadians to become more familiar with their own country, provided them with the means and facilities to explore it, promoted the arts and cultural development and even to a degree helped to influence the most compelling of all Canadian concerns, national unity.

THE CANADIAN PACIFIC

Stoney Creek Bridge, Selkirk Mountains

THE NEW HIGHWAY TO THE ORIENT

ACROSS THE Mountains, Prairies and Rivers of CANADA.

William Cornelius Van Horne (center); Van Horne, at front center, and other CPR officials often toured the line to view the progress of improvements (top left); Summer track built outside of the snowsheds resurrected the ticket-selling views of the Selkirks (top right); A CPR crew with a snowplough ready to swing into action (bottom left); Snowshed construction in the Selkirks (bottom right)

I: Preparing The Way

William Cornelius Van Horne was an impressive man. Impressive not only in physical stature, but also in his ability to construct, operate and make profits from railways. He had begun his career as a telegraph operator, but had quickly gone on to hold several important positions with midwest American railways. In 1881 he was thirty-eight and held the challenging post of general superintendent of the Chicago, Milwaukee & St. Paul Railroad. At the end of that year he accepted the offer of the CPR Syndicate to become general manager of the Canadian Pacific Railway and began an amazing feat of construction on its line, melding together scattered pieces of government-built track, pushing track-laying crews to a record-setting pace and helping to allay the fears of hostile Indians and worried creditors alike.

The line was completed in 1885 but much of it was far from being operational. Parts of the roadbed remained unballasted; sidings, stations and watertanks remained to be constructed; and much of the line was in imminent danger of destruction from avalanches, mudslides or the collapse of hastily built trestlework. The railroad had to be safe, efficient and comfortable before it could attract passengers, especially the type of passenger much sought after as the one most likely to be paying money-making first-class fares — the tourist. The company president, George Stephen, had promised as much to the shareholders and set a tight deadline. In his 1884 report, delivered in June, 1885, Stephen stated that by the spring of 1886 the line would "be finished and in perfect condition, thoroughly equipped, possessing every requisite facility for doing its work economically and efficiently, and at least equal to the best of its competitors in all respects."

Van Horne quickly went to work to bring the line up to snuff. It was a costly matter: $6.2 million in 1886 alone, more than half of it in the mountains between Calgary and the Pacific coast. Problems in the east — ballasting, widening cuts and upgrading bridges — paled in comparison with the avalanche hazard in the west. The danger of the snowy torrents thundering down from the high peaks of the Selkirks had been known by the time the line was completed, their devastation having been noted during construction. Van Horne stationed observation teams in the Selkirks over the winter of 1885-86 and was stunned by their reports in the spring. One of the teams recorded nine avalanches covering one section of track and another calculated that some parts were buried up to thirty-nine feet. The solution was one that Van Horne was undoubtedly familiar with; in 1868-69 the Central Pacific Railway had built thirty-seven miles of snowsheds in the Sierras, and the Canadian Pacific would need more than thirty such sheds to cover some five miles of track. Several of the many designs used required cribwork filled with rock, and in 1886 alone the task consumed over 17½ million board feet of sawn or hewn timber, 1.1 million lineal feet of timbers and pilings and over $1,400,000. Further work proved necessary in 1887 and by 1888 there were fifty-three sheds in place complemented by a series of glance-works that deflected the avalanche in the desired direction.

Once this work was completed the track was much safer but over five miles of the ticket-selling views in the Selkirks, particularly those of the magnificent Great [Illecillewaet] Glacier, had been lost. Unwilling to accept the loss, Van Horne built an extra track outside the confines of the sheds to be used in summer. Other problems related to winter snows had to be overcome to ensure the safety of passengers. To rescue trains from entrapment by blizzards, special locomotives fitted with winged snowploughs were stationed at strategic locations ready to swing into action with a track-clearing crew on short notice. Similarly, emergency precautions were taken by stocking baggage cars with boxes of provisions containing such staples as cheese, biscuits, tea, sugar, corned beef and condensed milk. A report given at the meeting of the American Society of Engineers in 1888 also alluded to the existence of provision magazines established every ten to twelve miles and to storage dumps for emergency heating fuel to warm stranded passenger cars.

Given the magnitude of these and the numerous other problems to be faced before the line could be declared safe for passenger traffic, it was quite amazing that the service could meet Stephen's deadline and be inaugurated when it was — June 28, 1886. In truth, there were still some very questionable sections. One was the Big Hill near Field where the line descended into the Kicking Horse Valley at a grade of 4.4%, twice the usual allowable maximum, requiring the placement of three uphill escape tracks at key locations to stop any runaways.

Particularly worrisome was the section built on a government contract between Kamloops and Yale by Andrew Onderdonk; company engineers felt it was not up to standard. However, this problem became a political football and it was several years before it was rectified to the railway's satisfaction. Despite such shortcomings the CPR assured passengers in all its advertising that the line was completely safe.

These safety hazards made it difficult for the railway to be efficient in its first few years of operation. Its drive to maintain schedules included the adoption of a system of standard time invented by the CPR's former chief engineer, Sandford Fleming, in the early eighties. In this system timetables were drawn up using a twenty-four-hour clock instead of the usual twelve-hour a.m. and twelve-hour p.m. notations. Train crews were placed under strict discipline to adhere to schedules, something that had been less highly stressed in the past. A Canadian cleric and early traveller on the line, Dean James Carmichael of Montreal, pointed this out and commented favourably on the effect:

The third blessing of the C.P.R. revolution is punctuality. The day has past when express trains pulled up to allow officials to pick blackberries or to "liquor up," when travellers waited five to ten hours at leading stations, or built up fires in a box stove in the waiting-room of a way station, or lay full-stretched on a form, with a portmanteau for a pillow. These are memories of the past....I only know that the C.P.R. serpent started from Montreal sharp at 8.20 p.m., arrived sharp at North Bay 9.55 on the second day, touched every way station timed to the very minute — reached Winnipeg on time, reached Banff on time, reached North Bend on time, and steamed into Vancouver sharp at 1.30 p.m., leaving a

trail behind it of two thousand nine hundred and eighty-six miles, with a correct record all the way along.

If Van Horne was intractable on any point concerning passenger traffic it was comfort. At the inauguration of transcontinental service there were three classes of passage, colonist, second-class and first-class. The cheapest ticket was colonist, which provided accommodation in a colonist sleeping car (sometimes referred to as an emigrant car), which was basic but serviceable. A contemporary observer found them "comfortably seated, well ventilated and with reasonable arrangements for sleeping." Generally speaking, these cars were fitted out with upper and lower berths, as were other sleeping cars, but for ease in cleaning and disinfecting were not upholstered and the passenger either had to supply his own bedding or purchase it from a company agent at terminal stations. They were mainly intended for the flood of immigrants that the CPR's opening of the west had attracted from overseas. Second-class passage was merely a glorified version of colonist, the cars being essentially the same but with a different designation for those who did not wish to be identified as immigrants. First-class passage was Van Horne's major concern and here he was determined to provide the best that the railroad world could offer.

The standard for excellence in first-class travel had been established by George M. Pullman of Chicago who, as early as 1864, had recognized the profit to be made out of providing railway passengers with comfort. That year he had made two important contributions to comfortable, convertible day-night railway accommodation, the hinged upper berth that could be folded into the ceiling of the car and hinged seats and backs that could be made into lower berths. From these creations he had gone on to design luxurious parlour cars with rich upholstery, rugs, hangings and inlaid panelling and equally elegant dining cars where passengers (first-class, of course) took sumptuous meals prepared by Pullman's own chefs and served by his own waiters. In fact, everything Pullman provided was leased from his company and from their inception western American lines had contracted his equipment and staff. Van Horne, when he was a railway superintendent in the United States, had broken with tradition and had purchased and operated his own dining cars, feeling that it was more profitable to do so than to pay the high lease rates of the Pullman company.

Convinced that he had made the right decision, Van Horne decided that the CPR would own all its sleeping, parlour and dining cars from the outset. Many of these cars were built by the Barney and Smith Company of Dayton, Ohio, to his personal specifications. He stipulated, for example, that berths in the sleeping cars should be longer and wider than those found in the Pullman cars. An advertisement described these cars in glowing terms:

Particular attention is called to the PARLOR and SLEEPING-CAR SERVICE, So Important An Accessory Upon A Railway Whose Cars Are Run Upward Of Three Thousand Miles Without Change.

These cars are of unusual strength and size, with berths, smoking and toilet accommodations correspondingly roomy. Each transcontinental sleeping-car is provided with BATHROOMS, and all are fitted with double doors and windows to exclude the dust in the summer and the cold in the winter.

The seats are richly upholstered, with high backs and arms, and the central sections are made into luxurious sofas during the day.

The upper berths are provided with windows and ventilators, and have curtains separate from those of the berths underneath. The exteriors are of polished mahogany, and the interiors are of white mahogany and satinwood, elaborately carved; while the lamps, brackets, berth-locks, and other pieces of metal work are of old brass of antique design.

Accommodation in these parlour and sleeping cars was sold separately from passage and was available only to those holding first-class tickets. The cost of either an upper or lower berth for the entire trip from Montreal to the Pacific coast was $20.00 over and above the price of basic first-class transportation while the cost of a parlour car seat was half this amount.

Van Horne took every opportunity to boast about this equipment, as in an 1887 letter to General Washburn of Minneapolis who obviously had questioned the CPR's lack of Pullman equipment:

If you ever travelled by the Canadian Pacific, I think you would have a different opinion as to the Pullman service being better than any other. We take great pride in believing that our service is infinitely more popular with the travelling public. We compete with the Pullman Company...and wherever we come in competition our cars take the greater part of the business. It is to the vast superiority of our sleeping car service that our large transcontinental passenger business during the past year has been mainly due.

Equal attention was paid to comfort and service in the company's dining cars, also modelled on the Pullman cars. The CPR dining cars offered ornate decoration, tooled leather benches and the best in linen and silverware. Advertising for the dining car service was similar to that for the parlour and sleeping cars:

THE CANADIAN PACIFIC RAILWAY DINING CARS Excel in Elegance of Design and Furniture and in the Quality of Food and Attendance Anything Hitherto Offered To TRANSCONTINENTAL TRAVELLERS.

The fare provided in these cars is the best procurable and the cooking has a wide reputation for excellence. Local delicacies such as trout, prairie hens, antelope steaks, Fraser River salmon, succeed one another as the train moves westward.

The wines are of the company's special importation, and are of the finest quality.

Meals in the dining car were advertised at seventy-five cents during the first years of transcontinental service.

One of the important offshoots of the dining car service was the CPR hotel system, a key development in much of the company's future tourist success. Many travellers on transcontinental trains could ill-afford the cost of dining car meals and it became common for restaurants to spring up at divisional points where a quick and cheap meal could be obtained while the locomotive was being changed, watered or fuelled. These restaurants were usually privately operated but the railway had to establish its own restaurants in the mountains where it was impractical to haul the extremely heavy dining cars over the steep grades.

Work on such restaurant stops began in the spring of 1886 at three key locations, the Mount Stephen House at Field in the Kicking Horse Valley, the Glacier House at the foot of the Illecillewaet Glacier near Rogers Pass and the Fraser Canyon House at North Bend. The westbound Pacific Express and the eastbound Atlantic Express were timed to arrive at these points at mealtimes. Although they were not ready for operation when the first transcontinentals went through, temporary quarters in the form of dining cars pulled to the side of the tracks were used until the work was completed. All three of the buildings were designed by Thomas Sorby, an English architect living in Victoria, using similar plans embodying three storeys in the centre, two storeys on one wing and one storey on the other.

The only difference was that the plan of the Mount Stephen House was the reverse of the other two and it contained two dining rooms instead of one. When completed the buildings incorporated six or seven bedrooms, the Mount Stephen House beginning to receive guests in the fall of 1886 and the other two the following summer. According to his biographer, Walter Vaughan, Van Horne took a direct part in the design of the facilities: "The company's charter permitted it to operate hotels, and Van Horne now began to realize a long-held dream by starting a system of picturesque hotels commanding the choicest views in the Rockies and Selkirks. He found recreation and delight in sketching, suggesting, or modifying the elevations and plans of these structures." The finished products were rather charming, bearing some resemblance to Swiss buildings with clapboard siding, except for shingled second storeys, and ornamental carving under the eaves and windows. The Swiss appearance was deliberate, planned to fit in with what would become a "Swiss" or "Canadian Alps" advertising theme for the CPR's mountain promotional material. As to colour, an early visitor to Glacier House described it quite well: "The Glacier House is a very artistic building of the Swiss chalet type, coloured, externally, chrome yellow, relieved by dark brown beams and mouldings...."

Van Horne believed that the company should not manage the dining stations itself, although he did not feel that one party could manage them all satisfactorily. He was, however, convinced that the service and food had to be up to the standard set by the CPR's own dining cars, a goal that proved to be somewhat elusive. When the hotels opened they were all under the management of company men. This changed in 1887 when James Wharton, manager at Glacier House, was moved to Mount Stephen House and Glacier House was taken over on a contract basis by H.A. Perley, a former chief steward on the Allan Line of steamships. The terms of this contract show that the company was serious about providing the best for its passengers:

...the said Perley to manage for his own benefit and advantage their Hotel known as "The Glacier House," and its appurtenances, the Company to make no charge for the use of the house and premises, and the said Perley to have the receipts from the Hotel and Lunch Rooms, as his sole remuneration for keeping the same....

Glacier House, one of the company's three mountain "Hotel Dining Stations," under construction in 1886, just prior to the arrival of the first transcontinental train. O. Klotz photograph

Perley to manage their Hotel in such a way as to give entire satisfaction to the Company...and shall keep their Hotel and its immediate surroundings neat and clean; and shall employ a first-class cook and competent waiters who shall be kept neat and clean as to dress and otherwise; and who shall be civil and attentive to the guests; shall serve meals to passengers and guests in the best style and so as to give entire satisfaction to the travelling public; all meals in the first-class dining room to be charged for at the rate of seventy-five cents each, and the lodgings in the Hotel at the rate of One dollar per day....

The object and intent of this arrangement is to secure the keeping by said Perley of a strictly first-class Hotel Dining Station in the very best style.

Unfortunately, Van Horne soon began to receive complaints about the service. He sent James Sheffield, superintendent of sleeping, parlor and dining cars, to investigate and quickly made it clear in a letter to Harry Abbott, general superintendent of the Pacific Division, that such a state of affairs could not be tolerated, even though Perley was often overtaxed by the simultaneous arrival of the Pacific and Atlantic Expresses, one or the other, or both, running late:

Referring to your two letters about the Glacier House. First, as to the attendance at table. My telegram was not based upon Mr. Sheffield's report, but at least upon a dozen complaints which have been made here by passengers within the last two months. I asked Mr. Sheffield, especially, when he went west to look into this matter, and his own experience seems to fully confirm the reports that have been made. He stated that the

Staff of the Fraser Canyon House stand ready to receive patrons in 1887. Thomas Sorby's design features emulating a Swiss chalet are evident. William McFarlane Notman photograph

two trains met at the Glacier House, as I remember, on both occasions when he was there, and that he learned that they frequently met there. He said that he spoke to Mr. Perley about the inadequate table service, and that Mr. Perley replied that he had provided all the help he could afford to do. Whether he can afford it or not the passengers must be properly attended to even if we have to take the house into our hands in the end to do it.

If by reason of two trains meeting at the Glacier House, or if by reason of an unusual number of passengers on the train the passengers cannot get their meals within the timetable, the trains should be held until they can, for nothing creates so much dissatisfaction with a railway as to compel the passengers to go without their meals. Passengers should in every case be informed by the men in charge of the dining stations that they will have ample time for their meals and that the train will not leave without sufficient notice. This is not done, I believe, at Glacier or at North Bend, and in the absence of such notice, the movement of the train for some purpose has in a number of cases resulted in a stampede from the dining room.

Van Horne was also facing problems at the company-run hotels, which were proving to be extremely costly to operate:

There can be no good reason for the results shown at North Bend and Field. The hotel at Field, in addition to being excessively expensive, is very badly managed. I have never yet seen a decent meal in the house, and complaints are very numerous from passengers. One of these hotels should be run with a force not exceeding that of a dining car, and possibly with one man less in the kitchen, and with the facilities they have for taking care of the meats, provisions, etc. I am unable to see why the house should not alone be run without loss, but the year around should afford a profit.

As if to back up his statement about the hotel being run with a staff complement the size of a dining car crew he soon afterwards gave the responsibility for the new hotel system to Sheffield.

Undaunted by the initial problems with the hotels, Van Horne proceeded to build others. The first of these was in the boom town of Vancouver, the Pacific terminus for the CPR after the extension of the line from the original terminus of Port Moody in 1887. The recommendation to build the hotel to serve the future needs of CPR passengers disembarking at Vancouver came from the general manager in February, 1886, just as the new town was beginning to scratch a place out of the heavy timber of Burrard Inlet. There was also a promise by the company to build the hotel as part of a land grant to it in the new townsite. Construction began in July, 1886, shortly after a disastrous fire wiped out almost all of what was Vancouver at the time. Thomas Sorby had been commissioned to design a luxury hotel costing half a million dollars, but when it was completed in May, 1888, he claimed that it had been built "without the architecture." Many agreed, one observer calling the four-storey brick building with steep-pitched tile roofs "an exceedingly ugly workhouse or asylum-looking structure." A somewhat kinder critic remembered it as "a solid, rather plain structure, a sort of glorified farmhouse, to which a number of extra storeys had been added."

While the Hotel Vancouver was simple and utilitarian, Van Horne's other hotel scheme of the period was quite the opposite. Recognizing the tourist potential of the hot springs near the station of Banff in the Rocky Mountains, which the federal government had just reserved for public use, he determined to build a hotel devoted entirely to serving every need and whim of the traveller. As a site he chose a magnificent promontory above the confluence of the Bow and Spray Rivers overlooking the Bow Valley with a view toward the Fairholme Range, and as an architect he chose one of the foremost of the day, Bruce Price of New York. Price had already been commissioned early in 1886 to design the CPR's new combined railway station and office building in Montreal, the impressive Windsor Station. Soon afterwards Van Horne asked him to prepare drawings for the Banff hotel and later that summer Price submitted plans that had their inspiration in the sixteenth-century chateaux of the Loire Valley in France. In choosing this style Price united the sense of luxury that Van Horne desired with a design that he felt was appropriate to the mountainous environment. Van Horne had been severely conscious of the costs of constructing the company's previous hotels, but Price operated under no such strictures for he later reported that he had "the entire resources of the Canadian Pacific Railway to draw upon, and hence it was possible to build with certain materials in certain ways." Draw upon them he did as the cost of the completed structure was about a quarter of a million dollars, a large sum for the times, reportedly amassed by the sale of some of the company's lots in Vancouver.

Work on the foundation excavation began in the winter of 1886-87 and construction was started in the spring of 1887 by a crew of several hundred CPR workers. When Van Horne stopped off in Banff in the summer of 1887 to check on progress he found, to his horror, that the plans had been turned 180 degrees, the kitchen overlooking the magnificent view and the rotunda facing the wooded slopes of Sulphur Mountain. Utilizing his own considerable architectural skills, he immediately worked up a sketch for a new rotunda pavilion attached to the kitchen, saving the view for the guests rather than the help.

Finishing work was completed on the interior over the following winter and by early summer of 1888 all was in readiness for the opening. Van Horne christened the creation the Banff Springs Hotel, in reference to the nearby hot springs, and declared that it was the "Finest Hotel on the North American Continent." While some well-travelled patrons may have had reservations about this statement, few would have denied that it was one of the finest or that it had the most spectacular location. In appearance it consisted of two frame wings each five storeys high, the top storey actually forming

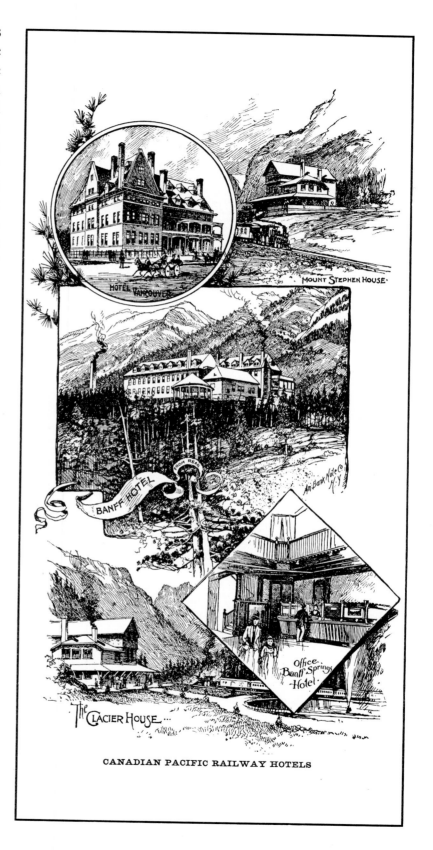

CANADIAN PACIFIC RAILWAY HOTELS

The *Abyssinia* arrives at Vancouver on June 14, 1887 carrying the CPR's first steamship passengers

Main lobby of the Banff Springs Hotel with overhanging balconies. A. B. Thom photograph

to railway construction camps on the north shore of Lake Superior. Henry Beatty of the North-West Transportation Company was recruited to head the CPR's Lake Transportation Service in 1882, in time to oversee the building of three 2,300-ton steel passenger-cargo steamers, the *Alberta*, *Algoma* and *Athabasca*, on the Clyde. When put into service out of Owen Sound in 1884 they were, pending the completion of the railway north of Lake Superior, the only connection for passengers travelling from Montreal to points west of the lakehead as far as the end of track. Even with the beginning of transcontinental rail service, the "Great Lakes" or "Thunder Bay Route" remained a popular alternative for tourists wishing to avoid the rather tedious train trip north of Lake Superior.

But the accomplishments on the Great Lakes were minor in comparison with George Stephen's vision of CPR ocean service. From the very beginning of his involvement with the CPR he had dreamed of it as part of an all-British route extending from England to the Orient. In 1882 the company even issued a map showing a projected steamship connection from the completed rail-line on the Pacific to Japan and Hong Kong. Stephen visited England in 1884 in an effort to convince the Colonial Office and the Post Office that a mail contract awarded to the CPR could result in a combined steamship and rail service that would allow faster delivery than the standard all-water route from the Orient through the Suez Canal. Unhappily, when tenders for such a service were advertised in October, 1885, the CPR's bid was not accepted, thereby dashing hopes that a joint passenger and mail service would be in place to join the new transcontinental rail service. Subsequently the company chartered sailing ships to carry cargo from the Orient to its Pacific terminus, the barque *W.B. Flint* being the first to arrive at Port Moody in July, 1886, carrying over a million pounds of tea. Sailing ships were later followed by chartered steamships that could carry both cargo and passengers. The 3,600-ton *Abyssinia* sailed from Hong Kong to Yokohama in May, 1887, with twenty-two first-class and eighty Chinese steerage passengers, arriving in Vancouver on June 14, just three weeks after the first passenger train had arrived at the new terminus. Other passenger-carrying chartered steamers soon followed, but Stephen's dream of a company steamship line forming part of an all-British route would have to wait.

part of the dormered roof, with Van Horne's pavilion jutting out towards the river. Like its companion mountain hotels it was finished in a cream colour and incorporated cedar shingles to good advantage. The main feature of the interior was the lobby, an octagonal rotunda that had overhanging balconies on successive floors allowing a view down to the main floor from each level. Other features included parlours, dining rooms, smoking rooms, a reading room and, for the gentlemen, a billiard room and bar. When the hotel opened its doors in June it was under the management of George Holliday and advertised rates from $3.50 a day upwards.

One further tourist-related service that both Stephen and Van Horne had hoped to have in place by the time transcontinental trains started running was an ocean steamship passenger line. The CPR first became involved with ships in 1883 when steamers were used to carry supplies from Owen Sound on Georgian Bay to the head of the Great Lakes at Port Arthur and

The Marquis of Lorne's article *Our Railway To The Pacific*, reprinted as a pamphlet in 1886, holds the distinction of being the CPR's first piece of tourist promotional literature

With equipment and facilities in place and the line successfully operating, it remained for the CPR to attract the travelling public, an endeavour in which Van Horne became personally involved through the Passenger Traffic Department. Most North American railroads left the job of organizing passenger traffic in the hands of a passenger agent but Van Horne decided that its importance required someone to coordinate all its various aspects. Consequently, he created the position of passenger traffic manager, the first on the continent, and recruited the capable Lucius Tuttle, formerly general passenger and ticket agent for the Boston & Lowell Railroad, to fill it. Assisting him were David McNicoll, general passenger agent in the Montreal headquarters, and Robert Kerr, freight and passenger agent, Western and Pacific Divisions in Winnipeg. The purpose of the department was twofold: to create the possibilities for passenger travel through the arrangement of schedules, the establishment of fares, the provision of tickets and the handling of baggage, and to persuade the traveller to partake of these possibilities. At the grass-roots level the fulfillment of the second purpose was handled by the agent, who solicited or "worked up" traffic by selling passage, attempting to interest the customer in sleeping or parlour car tickets, arranging hotel accommodation and looking after the many other details that would ensure him an enjoyable and worry-free journey. Depending on the size of the office where he worked, the agent could have a variety of titles, extending from station agent in small locales to town ticket agent in somewhat larger centres to city passenger agent in major Canadian cities. Complementing these agents was the travelling passenger agent whose job it was to assist them when required, to meet representatives of groups wanting to organize travel, to accompany special groups personally and to make arrangements with other carriers to complete a travel itinerary when required.

Half the company's complement of twelve travelling passenger agents in 1889 worked with agents representing the CPR in the United States. American agents too operated under numerous titles depending on their location and responsibilities, varying from the general eastern agent in New York City to the commercial agent in Chicago to the freight and passenger agent in Philadelphia. Passenger business in Great Britain and on the European Continent was handled initially by the CPR Emigration Department and later in the eighties by the European traffic agent, Archer Baker, with offices in London, Liverpool and Glasgow. Further afield solicitation was placed in the hands of travel agencies such as Thomas Cook & Son or others using its very successful commission formula. Countries where travel agencies acted for the CPR by the early nineties included Australia (Oceanic S. S. Co.), Japan (Frazar & Co.), India and Burma (Thomas Cook), and Ceylon and China (Jardine, Matheson & Co.).

Van Horne himself directed the advertising campaign to attract passengers. Again taking a page from his American experience, he applied his limited funds to newspaper and journal advertising, the production of posters and the writing and illustrating of promotional brochures and pamphlets. George Ham, the journalist who later headed the first CPR publicity department, recounted in his memoirs *Reminiscences of a Raconteur* Van Horne's first efforts in this direction and the reception they received:

When the passenger service of the C.P.R. was inaugurated the citizens of Montreal, Toronto, Ottawa and other large centres were puzzled and astonished one morning on seeing numerous billboards decorated with streamers on which were printed: "Said the Prince to the Duke: 'How high we live on the C.P.R.'" and "What the Duke said to the Prince: 'All sensible people travel on the C.P.R.'" "Parisian Politeness on the C.P.R." "Great Salome on the C.P.R." "Wise Men of the East Go West on the C.P.R." and "By Thunder — Bay passes the C.P.R.," the final four words of the latter being in comparatively small type.

They created quite a little stir at the time, being something novel in advertising. Twenty-five years later an advertising man recalled the advertisements and gave his opinion that they were no good, and also intimated that they were really quite idiotic. "And yet you remember them for a quarter of century?" I asked. "They must have been pretty good advertising." *And they were.*

CPR ticket office on Vancouver's Granville Street, 1892

settlement guide *The Great Prairie Provinces of Manitoba and the Northwest Territories*. Soon afterwards it began to distribute tens of thousands of maps, folders and pamphlets in ten languages to agencies all over Britain and Continental Europe. Coordinating its activities out of its London office, the department published ads regularly in 167 British and 147 Continental journals and newspapers. The way was therefore well prepared and it may be accurately stated that the CPR's tourist promotion was launched on the back of its well-oiled emigration campaign.

The CPR's London office was ideally situated at 88 Cannon Street, near the Cannon Street station of the South Eastern Railway, and on the way to the London Bridge station, served by the South Eastern and the London, Brighton & South Coast Railway. It has been estimated that three-quarters of a million people passed by this office, which was also close to London Bridge and St. Paul's Cathedral, each day. From this unparalleled pedestrian flow there were undoubtedly many who wanted to see something of the rest of the world. Initially the only problem stemmed from a lack of promotional material with which to attract them. Realizing this, Begg, working on Van Horne's instructions, began designing a small pamphlet to

Creations of this nature, however, were not enough to attract what was by this time a fairly sophisticated travelling public. Van Horne and his passenger traffic staff realized that better techniques and more in-depth promotional materials were needed to gain their attention. It was the CPR's tourist and immigration literature, both artfully illustrated, that gave many non-Canadians and, indeed, many Canadians their first knowledge of the recently-opened Canadian west. While the hook to attract immigrants was the enormous agricultural potential of Canada, the attention-grabber for tourists was the great natural wonders to be found in the Canadian landscape, particularly those in the mountains. Thus the generation and distribution of this promotional material was to become the second phase in Van Horne's scheme to "capitalize the scenery."

If Canada was to become part of an all-British route to the Orient, as both he and Stephen hoped, it was vital that a flow of British tourists be induced. And the British were ripe for the picking. Most Britons liked to travel in the Empire (as one put it when speaking of the United States, "their ways are not our ways") and many were aware through newspaper and journal reports of the building of the Canadian line. Also in Great Britain the network through which agents could promote tourism and distribute literature was already in place by the time they began their work. Alexander Begg's Emigration Department had launched its campaign to sell CPR lands in western Canada as early as 1881 with the distribution of the

provide a stopgap until a more substantial offering could be produced. This first pamphlet was to take the form of a reproduction of an article by the Marquis of Lorne, the former Governor-General of Canada, which had originally been written for the English journal *Good Words*. On May 11, 1886, Begg wrote to Van Horne: "I hope to have the reproduction of the Marquis of Lorne's article on 'Our Railway to the Pacific' ready in a day or two…and expect that when it is issued I shall be in a position…of doing something practical in working up tourist business this summer and fall." When the pamphlet appeared it was tastefully illustrated with engravings from drawings by Lorne's wife, Princess Louise, and was full of praise for the men who had built the CPR, the settlement possibilities it opened up in the Canadian west and, above all, its scenic beauties and tourist potential:

> *The task is done, and done in less time than many governments would take to talk of it. The Canadian Pacific Railway spans the continent. Nowhere can finer scenery be enjoyed from the window of a car than upon this line. There is no doubt that the favourite Transatlantic excursion will no longer be to New York, Niagara, Montreal and Quebec only, but that all who have a month's time to spend will go to the Pacific by the Northern American line, or come back that way, making the Canadian Pacific Railway their object on the outward or return journey.*

Joining the Lorne pamphlet during the first year of transcontinental passenger traffic operation was the annotated timetable, a hand-out that was tremendously popular with tourists over the years. The first transcontinental time-table was issued to coincide with the inauguration of service (a souvenir version appeared on yellow Oriental silk), along with the famous "Red Letter Day" poster announcing the start of daily service (except Sunday) beginning on June 28, 1886, from Toronto, Montreal and Ottawa for the Pacific Ocean. The timetable listed the stations reached as the train proceeded west and their mileage from both Montreal and Vancouver as well as the scheduled time of arrival and departure. Other columns, which had to be read from bottom up, allowed the passenger to use the timetable on a train running from west to east. Because of

SIR DONALD AND THE GREAT GLACIER OF THE SELKIRKS

the popularity of the timetable with passengers and their requests for more information, the railway immediately decided to produce fuller versions.

The annotated timetable added a narrative description of the trip. Typically the text for eastern Canadian points dwelled on the history, industrial and natural resource development and sporting opportunities of the passing countryside. In the Eastern Division (Montreal to Fort William) little was mentioned of tourist appeal except the attractions of major cities such as Montreal and Ottawa, the possibilities of connections to Niagara Falls through Toronto and the option of the steamship detour from Owen Sound to Port Arthur, adjoining Fort William at the lakehead. In the Western Division (Fort William to Donald, in the Columbia Valley) the emphasis began to change. Although it was the agricultural possibilities of the country that received the most attention, landscape began to become important at the Lake of the Woods, where "the scenery is of the wildest description, and deep rock-bound lakes are always in sight." Out on the prairies several comments were made about the beauty of the wide vistas, but it was not until Gleichen, where the first view of the mountains could be obtained, that the emphasis shifted to the description of scenery and the outlining of tourist possibilities, and it continued in this vein to the end of the Western Division and throughout the Pacific Division (Donald to Vancouver). All the best adjectives were brought out to describe the breathtaking surroundings, and the words of a notable traveller, Agnes Macdonald, wife of the Prime Minister, were borrowed to good effect in a subsequently oft-used advertising technique, the testimonial. The timetable quoted Lady Macdonald, nearing Banff aboard a special train in July, 1886 (on which she rode a good deal of the way through the mountains seated on the cowcatcher):

Here the pass we are travelling through has narrowed suddenly to four miles, and as mists float upwards and away, we see great masses of scarred rock rising on each side — ranges towering one above the other. Very striking and magnificent grows the prospect as we penetrate into the mountains at last, each curve of the line bringing fresh vistas of endless peaks rolling away before and around us, all tinted rose, bluish-pink and silver, as the sun lights their snowy tips. Every turn becomes a fresh mystery, for some huge mountain seems to stand right across our way, barring it for miles, with a stern face frowning down upon us; and yet a few minutes later we find the giant has been encircled and conquered, and soon lies far away in another direction.

While the description of Ottawa, the nation's capital, was restricted to less than half a page, the description of Banff occupied almost a page and a half and included information on Rocky Mountains Park, the names of the mountains seen from the station, surrounding lakes, the new Banff Springs Hotel and the hot springs. Equal amounts of space were devoted to descriptions at each of the Rocky Mountain stations but it was in the Selkirks that the scenery and attractions received the highest accolades. At Glacier House, the Illecillewaet Glacier was described as "a vast plateau of gleaming ice extending as far as the eye can reach, as large, it is said, as all those of Switzerland combined," while Mount Sir Donald, the premier peak of the area, "rises, a naked and abrupt pyramid, to a height of more than a mile and a half above the railway."

Man's creations as well as God's received due attention. Like the Illecillewaet Glacier, the hotel was promoted in a manner that called to mind Switzerland, a ploy that was to become a hallmark of CPR mountain advertising: "The hotel is a handsome structure, resembling a Swiss chalet, which serves not only as a dining-station for passing trains, but affords a most delightful stopping place for tourists who wish to hunt, or explore the surrounding mountains or glaciers." Similarly, the

A passenger train emerges from one of the CPR's engineering feats, a snowshed, onto another, the Loop. Vaux family photograph

company's engineering feats were noted as attractions in themselves: the Loop, where the line was described as doubling back upon itself "within a biscuit's toss;" the Stoney Creek bridge, "one of the loftiest railway bridges in the world;" the square-timbered snowsheds that "bid defiance to the most terrific avalanche;" and, at Albert Canyon, the "solidly built balconies which enable passengers to safely look into the boiling cauldron below."

Interleaved copies of the annotated timetable were available on request so that eager tourists could make notes or memoranda on the wonders of Canada and the CPR as they went along. Copies of the ordinary timetable were usually issued as part of a larger production known as *Folder 'A' Canadian Pacific Railway*. Folder 'A' included, in addition to the ordinary timetable, a condensed timetable, a list of the general officers of the company, a list of agencies acting for the

The Pacific Express pauses to allow passengers to view the precipitous Albert Canyon from a specially built platform. Byron Harmon photograph

company, railway, steamship and stage connections at various points, facts, and a large "Map of the Canadian Pacific Railway and Its Connections."

It was apparent from the annotated timetable that the company's promotion of Canada was focused on the mountain west. This became even more obvious in the advertising material that soon joined it. In 1887 the high-quality, tourist-oriented pamphlet that Van Horne had been working on since 1884 finally appeared. The long delay in publication stemmed from Van Horne's insistence on the best possible illustrations. Also there was a strong suggestion that Van Horne himself had prepared the text and, because of his other duties, had found it difficult to meet a deadline.

The finished work, *The Canadian Pacific, The New Highway to the East Across the Mountains, Prairies & Rivers of Canada*, opened with a sport-and-scenery pitch to the upper-class English traveller:

May I not tempt you, kind reader, to leave England for a few short weeks and journey with me across that broad land, the beauties and glories of which have only now been brought within our reach? There will be no hardships to endure, no difficulties to overcome, and no dangers or annoyances whatever. You shall see mighty rivers, vast forests, boundless plains, stupendous mountains and wonders innumerable; and you shall see all in comfort, nay in luxury. If you are a jaded tourist, sick of Old World scenes and smells, you will find everything fresh and novel. If you are a sportsman, you will meet with unlimited opportunities and endless variety, and no

one shall deny you your right to hunt or fish at your sweet will. If you are a mountain climber, you shall have cliffs and peaks and glaciers worthy of your alpenstock, and if you have lived in India, and tiger hunting has lost its zest, a Rocky Mountain grizzly bear will renew your interest in life.

The same upper-class market was the target of description of the railway's passenger equipment. After mentioning the "bright and cheerful colonist coaches" for the comfort of "the hardy and good-looking emigrants" and the "handsomely fitted coaches" for the passengers making short trips, the narrative turned to "the sleeping cars or 'Pulmans'" for the first-class tourist:

The railway carriages to which you are accustomed are dwarfed to meet Old World conditions, but these in our train seem to be proportioned to the length and breadth of the land. Our sleeping car is unlike the 'Pullmans' you have seen in England, being much larger and much more luxurious. With its soft and rich cushions, silken curtains, thick carpets, delicate carvings and beautiful decorations, and with its numberless and ingenious appliances for convenience and comfort (even to the bath-room so dear to the travelling Englishman), it gives us promise of a delightful journey.

The narrator assumed that the tourist's main objective was the Rocky Mountains: "But you are impatient to see the mountains, and if you will permit me to choose, dear reader, we will start from Montreal by the main line of the railway, and in order that we may miss nothing we will return by the great lakes, and see Toronto and the Falls of Niagara then." Until the

Engraving depicting Rat Portage at the Lake of the Woods from the pamphlet *The New Highway to the East*

mountains were reached the description concentrated on the agricultural possibilities of the west and the sport to be found along the line. On the long haul north of Lake Superior "we are alert for the sight of a bear, a moose or a deer, and we do not heed the time. Our only regret is that we cannot stop for even an hour to cast a fly in one of the many tempting pools." Out on the prairies huge coveys of prairie chickens and large flocks of ducks and geese were seen and it was mentioned that most of the sportsmen had dropped off at stations along the way, with the exception of those who pushed on for larger game farther west, particularly antelope. To these wary animals the narrator paid particular attention, perhaps feeling they would prove to be somewhat exotic to the English sportsman: "Hour after hour we roll along with little change in the aspect of the country. The geese and ducks have ceased to interest us, and even a coyote no longer attracts attention; but the beautiful antelope has never-ending charm for us, and as, startled by our approach, he bounds away, we watch the white tuft which serves him as a tail until it disappears in the distance." According to the CPR, Canada was "a very paradise for sportsmen."

The mountains were described in terms similar to those in the annotated timetable:

Serrated peaks, and vast pyramids of rock with curiously contorted and folded strata, are followed by gigantic castellated masses down whose sides cascades fall thousands of feet. The marvellous clearness of the air brings out the minutest detail of this Titanic sculpture. Through the gorges we catch glimpses of glaciers and other strange and rare sights, and, now and then of wild goats and mountain sheep, grazing on the cliffs far above us near the snow line.

At Glacier House the description found in the annotated timetable was paraphrased and a new allusion to Switzerland coined: "Descending westerly from the summit we reach in a few minutes the Glacier House, a delightful hotel situated almost in the face of the Great Glacier and at the foot of the grandest of all the peaks of the Selkirks — Sir Donald — an acute pyramid of rock shooting up nearly eight thousand feet above us, a dozen Matterhorns in one." Again the Loop was mentioned and likewise range after range of mountains until the train entered the precipitous canyon of the Fraser where the view became somewhat terrifying:

Hundreds of feet above the river is the railway, notched into the face of the cliffs, now and then crossing a great chasm by a tall viaduct or disappearing in a tunnel through a projecting spur of rock, but so well made, and so thoroughly protected everywhere, that we feel no sense of danger. For hours we are deafened by the roar of the water below and pray for the broad sunshine once more. The scene is fascinating in its terror, and we finally leave it gladly, yet regretfully.

From this point to the coast the tenor of the description changed to emphasize similarities with England, making the tourist feel more at home after his awe-inspiring experiences in the mountains: "As the valley widens out farms and orchards become more and more frequent, and our hearts are gladdened with the sight of broom and gorse and other shrubs and plants familiar to English eyes, for as we approach the coast we find the climate like that of the south of England, but with more sunshine." And, to end the narrative, after disembarking at Vancouver and exploring the city, the tourist was invited to take a steamer to Vancouver Island, where he would find himself entirely at home: "A steamer will take you there in a few hours and you will be rewarded in finding a transplanted section of Old England, climate, people, and all, more vigorous, perhaps, because of the transplanting. Near Victoria you will find Esquimalt, the North Pacific Naval Station, and an iron-clad or two, and perchance some old friends from home; and let me advise you, furthermore, to take all of your baggage with you to Victoria, for I am sure you will be in no hurry to come away."

The New Highway to the East proved to be very appealing to those interested in travel passing the Cannon Street or other CPR offices in Great Britain and the company soon added companion pieces. One of these appealed to those who found their enjoyment in a more active style of life. Entitled *Fishing and Shooting On The Canadian Pacific Railway*, it was issued to attract the thousands of sportsmen eager to come to grips with the big game, small game and fish spread across Canada. *Fishing and Shooting* ultimately became the most popular piece of promotional literature ever issued by the CPR, running to more than thirty editions.

The pamphlet began with a double-barrelled claim: "No other part of the continent is on a par with Canada in the variety and plenty of sport obtainable at the expense of a little time and pleasant trouble; and it so happens that the best game

districts in the Dominion are either in the immediate vicinity [of], or at no great distance from, the Canadian Pacific Railway." It then turned to outlining the various parts of the country and the delights they had to offer sportsmen. Moose hunting in New Brunswick and fishing in Northern Ontario were described but again the emphasis on the west was apparent: "What are undoubtedly the finest shooting grounds to be found in America at the present day are enclosed within the boundaries of the Canadian Northwest." And again it was the mountains that were described as the mecca: "You want big game — stately elk, fierce bears, sneaky panthers, big-horned sheep, snowy goats, etc.? Very good. You can have them one and all, and caribou and deer to boot, providing you yourself are game to follow the guide." This last point was emphasized and the sportsman warned that he must be prepared to face some hardships to gain his trophy:

The pursuit of what is generally dubbed by the craft 'big game' in the mountain wilds of Canada is no child's play. To be successful, a man must possess iron nerve and unflinching determination; he must be a good shot, and strong enough to stand the rough work; for the latter is frequently necessary before the game can be reached, and the former is very liable to be an extremely useful accomplishment, especially if the quarry happens to be a grizzly bear....

Shooting the grizzly is other work. The big plantigrade is always looking for trouble, and when he digs up the hatchet he goes on the warpath. You will have no friendly elephant, nor army of beaters, to satisfy his craving for somebody's scalp. You start on his track, and follow him into his gloomy fastness amid a chaos of rocks, your life in one hand and your rifle in the other; and unless you are made of the right material, stop before the scent gets too hot, or peradventure you may be found empty-handed by your party.

However, this spice of dan---, or rather danger spiced with a chance of escape, is very fascinating; and, if you would fain be fascinated to your heart's content, seek the Rocky Mountains of British Columbia and enjoy your whim.

The writer knew that by throwing down the gauntlet in such a way the challenge would prove irresistible to many hunters who spent their lives in pursuit of dangerous game. To aid them in planning their trip, the pamphlet concluded with a listing of the closed seasons for fish and game in the provinces and

"Hunting in North-West Canada"

territories of Canada.

Concomitants to CPR advertising also helped to spread the word, many of these taking the form of articles in newspapers and magazines. However, a more substantial testimonial was a privately-printed brochure entitled *A Holiday Trip, Montreal to Victoria And Return Via the Canadian Pacific Railway, Mid-summer 1888*, which had a very exclusive appeal. It was an account of a trip taken by Richard White of Montreal, manager of *The Gazette*, his brother William White, QC, of Sherbrooke, and two Anglican divines, Canon John Empson, secretary of the Diocese of Montreal, and the Rev. James Carmichael, later Dean of Montreal. Carmichael, who acted as narrator, mentioned that the four travellers had agreed that the account should be printed at the expense of Richard White for private distribution. However, as a friend of Van Horne, White obtained company etchings, photographs and advertising for use as illustrations. The pamphlet was intended primarily for friends of the travellers, many of them in Great Britain, as was indicated early on: "For the benefit of friends in the Mother Country into whose hands this record may fall, it is necessary to say something about the two thousand nine hundred mile railroad on which we travelled."

Like its CPR counterpart *The New Highway to the East*, after which it was obviously modelled, Carmichael's *Holiday Trip* emphasized the benefits of travelling first-class:

Here again, for the benefit of Old-Country friends, let me say something as to the comforts of such a mode of travelling. The CPR inaugurated three elements in the comfort of passengers, hitherto largely unknown to the general Canadian public, namely: civility, punctuality and comfortable quarters for emigrant travellers. Railway porters or attendants on parlor or sleeping cars, up to the CPR revolution, were, as a rule, amongst the most irritating of Her Majesty's subjects, their manner constantly changing from the coolly impertinent to the servilely civil, the latter stage being reached as each despised passenger neared the close of his journey and shillings became the order of the day. Now all of this has changed. The civility, always characteristic of the CPR porter, has already influenced the conduct on other leading lines....

As for the "Sleeping" or first-class cars, one has only to travel a straight stretch of three thousand miles in one of them to give a verdict — all along the line — in their favor. Each car is a luxuriously finished drawing room, well ventilated and lighted, with large plate glass windows giving a wide field of vision — with bath-rooms and wash-rooms, and smoking-room, electric bells and hot air heating apparatus, and in the night, each compartment is changed into a sleeping room that one has only to get accustomed to, to rest soundly. Lasting luxury, cool comfort, such, in fine, is the CPR day car for the first-class passenger.

The pamphlet also paid tribute to the new Banff Springs Hotel and the Hotel Vancouver, both of which the party patronized. The Banff Springs was "palatial...with the grandest view of mountain scenery we could ask to see, lying at our feet, the valley of the Bow, hemmed in with its attendant mountains, a view that would repay a person for the whole journey." The Hotel Vancouver was "in every way a first-class house [which] gave us splendid accommodation."

As for the mountains, Carmichael was a bit overwhelmed, as many tourists were: "I never saw or hoped to see anything so awfully grand, and I suppose I could never feel again the same feelings in connection with the same view, though the sense of awfulness never wholly left me as long as ever we were under the shadows of those giant piles of rock...." The section he felt to be "the gem of the Rockies" was the Kicking Horse, where he related the experience of ascending to the pass and then descending down the canyon on the notorious Big Hill:

It would be altogether out of place, even if one could do it, to attempt to picture too closely the awful grandeur of this portion of our journey. The pass, up to which the engine climbs, as if straining every bolt and bar in it, stands at an altitude of five thousand two hundred and ninety-six feet, with wild bare masses of rock six thousand and ten thousand feet above our heads, and out before us. Up we go, the engine breathing like a hard-run man, until we reached the summit, where from a lake there issues the Kicking Horse Stream, which gradually grows into a river, and the maddest, the most passionate, the most uncontrollable river for its size that one could well find. Soon we glide into the great canyon, and begin to run down a gradient of one hundred and fifty to two hundred feet to the mile, above us the awful looking rocks, and far down below, the boiling, raging little river.

Lord Stanley and his party avail themselves of the opportunity provided many influential tourists – riding the cowcatcher – in 1889

After a stop at Glacier House, Carmichael expressed a desire to ride on the engine and, with Richard White, was granted the privilege, a fairly common occurrence for influential tourists who agreed to sign a waiver relieving the CPR of any liability. However, he quickly changed his mind "when I saw that 'on the engine' meant sitting on a hot iron seat with our feet hanging over the cowcatcher, and nothing to hold on to but a brass rod." He transferred his permission to William White and soon afterwards, as the train began to go through the Loop, he looked out to see how the brothers were doing: "Looking out from the back of the car, again and again I saw the Manager and the Judge holding on bravely as the engine rounded the curves, with nothing but the bare lines before them and the terrible trestles beneath. It may be a very nice thing to be a Q.C., or the manager of a leading paper, but as I saw these lights of the law and the press 'flying through the air' ahead of me, I really felt as if I would sooner be a Blackfoot Indian, with solid prairie under my feet, than either of those gentlemen graduating on a cowcatcher."

As mentioned, *A Holiday Trip*, like *The New Highway to the East* and *Fishing and Shooting*, was profusely illustrated, an aspect of CPR tourist promotion that was a significant exercise in image-making for both the company and the country. As such, it deserves fuller examination.

Watercolour artist F. M. Bell-Smith painting Mount Stephen from the shore of Wapta Lake in 1887. William McFarlane Notman photograph

III: The Railway Art School

The production of high-quality tourist pamphlets and brochures, replete with engravings and photographs, turned the CPR and its chief officers into leading patrons of Canadian art. Canadian artists had gone through a period of searching for a national focus, resulting in the formation of the Royal Canadian Academy of Artists in 1879 and the opening of the National Gallery soon afterwards. As early as 1876 an art critic had recognized that the great European artistic dedication to nature at its most sublime was affecting Canadian art, stating "that Canadian scenery has its own characteristics, and that the chief merit of our best artists is that they reproduce these with striking fidelity..." Fortunately this focus coalesced with the CPR's requirements for landscape material and also with the Canadian public's awakening spirit of nationalism and interest in the northwest spawned by the building of the transcontinental line. Comfortable with painting the forests, lakes and rivers and some of the natural wonders of eastern Canada, such as Niagara Falls and Percé, these artists were as yet unfamiliar with the rugged grandeur and the challenging light that awaited them in the new land. But aided by the company, they were soon dedicating themselves wholeheartedly to rendering the mountain west in its minutest detail. It may therefore be said that the CPR's requirements and its assistance played a key part in what may be called "the railway school," Canada's first "national" school of art.

Van Horne played a personal role in the creation of this school. As in the case of the written material for the pamphlets, he took a direct interest in the creation of illustrative pieces. Promotion was part of his responsibility when he became vice-president of the company in 1884 and he immediately became involved in the writing and designing of *The New Highway to the East*. The same year he commissioned the highly respected Montreal photographic firm of William Notman and Son to send a party to the west to photograph the prairies and the construction of the line through the Rockies,

undoubtedly with an eye toward including some of the views in this pamphlet. In the eighties half-tone reproductions of photographs first came into their own as illustrations in journals and books, and Van Horne intended that the CPR productions be the most up-to-date in every way.

The choice of the Notman firm to carry out this work was understandable. Shortly after establishing himself in Montreal in the late 1850s, William Notman gained both a national and international reputation for fine photography and progressive methods. Primarily a portrait photographer, he had turned to landscape photography about the time of Confederation and shortly afterwards received his first CPR commission. In 1871 Sandford Fleming, chief engineer of the then government-sponsored CPR, and Alfred Selwyn, director of the Geological Survey of Canada, combined forces to send a party over the proposed route of the newly announced transcontinental line. Headed by Selwyn, the party included two Notman employees, photographer Benjamin Baltzly and his assistant John Hammond. Setting out from Victoria, Selwyn intended to push through the Yellowhead Pass as far east as the fur trade depot of Jasper House, but bad weather conspired against them and the party eventually had to turn back near the pass. Despite poor atmospheric conditions for photography, Baltzly did manage to take 120 views on the trip, documenting the landscape through which it was intended the CPR would pass.

The next Notman photographer to head west in the interests of the CPR thirteen years later was Notman's own son, William McFarlane Notman, since 1882 a partner with his father in the firm. Van Horne supplied the younger Notman with an official car and in July he proceeded to the end of track in the Kicking Horse Valley and began to take a series of views of construction work and scenery in the vicinity. Added to these were several photographs of the prairies, probably taken at the end of the season while Notman was on his way back east. The quality of the photographs and the grandeur of the landscape they captured were evidently exactly what Van Horne required. By the fall of 1884 he had already put a selection of them in the hands of the American Bank Note Company, some to be made into half-tone photographic reproductions and others to be rendered by artists into engravings for the proposed pamphlet. In November he wrote to Thomas Lee of American Bank Note:

I have your favour of the 24th instant enclosing new proof view of Medicine Hat, in which you have made a very great improvement, the distance both in the foreground and in the plains beyond having been fully doubled...

As we will probably want to get out a guide book on a small scale before it would be possible to publish the large one contemplated — something to attract the attention of English Tourists our way before spring opens — we would like a few more engravings as soon as possible, and, therefore, without waiting to pass upon the "Mountains at Canmore," I will be glad if you will put in hand the following:

    Silver City and Castle Mountain 5 x 7¼
    Kicking Horse Valley Looking East 7 x 9
    Rat Portage (I enclose a new photograph for this) 4 x 7
    Flour mills and elevators — Portage La Prairie 3½ x 5
    Indian Head Station 2½ x 4
    Interior of the sleeping car

I will be glad if you let me know when we can count on being able to use these.

The view of Medicine Hat eventually appeared as a half-tone reproduction of a photograph in *The New Highway to the East* while the others mentioned appeared as engravings, made from the Notman photographs by American Bank Note artists. This process was accomplished by projecting the image onto the engraving block, which the artist would then follow in his design. Although the engraver could produce an almost exact copy in the engraving, he usually made small changes and embellishments to enhance the image. A comparison of the Notman photograph "Silver City and Castle Mountain, near Banff, Alberta, 1884" with the engraving "Silver City and Castle Mountain, Rocky Mountains" in *The New Highway to the East* provides a good example. Notman's photographs, while the first to be used for production of CPR advertising material, were by no means the only ones. Alexander Henderson was another extremely accomplished photographer

who, after the establishment of a studio in Montreal in the mid-1860s, became one of William Notman's chief competitors. Henderson has been described as "a genuine landscape artist" whose romantic view of nature and sensitive treatment of it led to the creation of a mood or aura in his work. This resulted in a strong reputation for him in art circles and he gained further note for his work from 1872 to 1874 documenting the construction of the Intercolonial Railway between Rivière du Loup and Halifax. Because of this he was known to Van Horne and was commissioned by the company in 1885 to carry on with the work begun by Notman in the west. Little is known of Henderson's trip except that he spent most of his time in the Selkirks near Rogers Pass capturing their grandeur

William McFarlane Notman's photograph "Silver City and Castle Mountain, near Banff, Alberta, 1884"

in his inimitable style. A third photographer, Professor Oliver B. Buell, a lecturer who toured North America and Europe giving travel programs illustrated with lantern slides, also travelled the main line with CPR sponsorship in 1885 and 1886.

Copies of Henderson's and Buell's photographs were lent by Van Horne to the artist John Fraser, who had studied at the Royal Academy in London before his family emigrated to Canada in 1858. On arriving in Montreal he had immediately gone to work for William Notman tinting photographs, and soon became the firm's art director. In 1868 he became Notman's partner in the new firm of Notman and Fraser established in Toronto and began to sell paintings as well as photographs. In April, 1873, his shop was the site of the first exhibition of the Ontario Society of Artists, an organization formed at his instigation in June, 1872. By 1879, the year he became one of the eight original nominees to the Royal Canadian Academy, he was regarded, along with Lucius O'Brien, as one of the foremost artists in the country. Unfortunately, he soon after had a falling out with O'Brien, who had been elected the first president of the RCA. Their dispute centred on the creation of *Picturesque Canada*, a two-volume production that began appearing in segments in 1882 containing engravings depicting the scenic wonders of the country. O'Brien became its art director and it was widely

Engraving in *The New Highway to the East* rendered from Notman's photograph

publicized that members of the RCA would carry out most of the 500 proposed illustrations. When it became apparent that American artists were receiving the bulk of the work, Fraser attacked both O'Brien and the Art Publishing Company, the American-backed publisher of the work. Because of O'Brien's position, Fraser became somewhat of an outsider, defensive about his work and suspicious of some of his fellow artists. Nevertheless his reputation was still very much intact when he wrote to Van Horne in 1885 concerning some illustrations for the contemplated CPR pamphlet.

The vice-president was himself a connoisseur of art, his personal collection eventually containing works of many recognized masters, and he may even be regarded as a very competent artist in his own right. He certainly would have known of Fraser, at least by reputation, and may have known him personally, as Fraser had been to the end of the line at Calgary in 1883. Furthermore, Fraser had already borrowed from the CPR a photograph by Buell of the mountains near Leanchoil to use as a reference for an engraving he was doing for *The Century Magazine*. This photograph was part of a portfolio that Buell had personally presented to Van Horne at Calgary during his return trip east from the Last Spike ceremony. Whatever their previous relationship, the October letter from Fraser set in motion an agreement that would be significant for both the CPR and Canadian art. It read:

Having read several times lately of the completion of the C.P.R. I am reminded of our conversation of last Nov. re. your contemplated guide book and I beg to say that I shall be glad to undertake the whole of the illustration work or a part of it. I could prepare many of the drawings and arts during the coming winter using photos you have and arrange for work in the field in the summer. Will you kindly favour me with an early communication stating your views, which I hope to be able to meet, and oblige.

Van Horne's reply has not been found, but judging from a further letter from Fraser to Van Horne's assistant, Arthur Piers, on November 25 it seems that he favoured the idea of using some of Fraser's work to complement that already in hand from Notman, Henderson and Buell. In the letter to Piers, Fraser referred to Van Horne's reply, which agreed to forward some views entitled "1. Rock slide & Debris. Great Glacier 2. East of Yale-near Sunset 3. Last Ray of sun on Mt. Stephen," presumably Henderson or Buell photographs. Then, in a letter dated January 6, 1886, Van Horne made another proposition:

Mr. Stephen, our President, is anxious that some large water colour views of our mountain scenery should be exhibited at the Colonial Exhibition, which is to be held in London next May. We have a quantity of photographic views here, new ones, which I presume would have to be depended on for material, as nothing could be done otherwise at this season of the year and Mr. Stephen will undertake to buy the pictures himself, if no better sale is made before the Exhibition closes.

If you would like to take this matter up, you had better

John Fraser produced a number of black and white sketches for tourist promotional use, including this view of the Banff Springs Hotel used in *A Holiday Trip*

come here without delay; but in any case let me know what you decide.

Fraser hastened at once to Montreal, where he collected the photographs. When the artist requested details of light and atmospheric conditions, Van Horne asked Henderson to supply the answers, which were forwarded to Fraser by Van Horne with this warning: "Please note what Mr. Henderson says about the wide angle lense lowering the mountains, and keep it in view as applying to all the views."

Carrying out this commission was to supersede the work that Fraser intended doing on the pieces for the advertising pamphlet. There were problems with the paintings since, as Fraser complained, they were already half completed using the lower proportions of the mountains when he found out Henderson's photographs had been taken with the wide lens. Fortunately, in a painting of Mount Stephen he had taken the liberty of raising the mountain somewhat above the proportions found in the photograph. The Mount Stephen picture and two others, one of Mount Hermit (in Rogers Pass) and one of Summit Lake (in Kicking Horse Pass), were completed in March, 1886, and were shipped to Van Horne for his approval before they were sent on to London for the exhibition. By then Fraser was ready to return to his work on the pamphlet.

The correspondence between Fraser and Van Horne on this matter reveals Van Horne's influence on art works used for advertising purposes. Since the company was unable to issue *The New Highway to the East* in time for the 1886 season Fraser was able to visit the mountains and work directly from the real scenery rather than photographs. This he did, leaving for the Pacific coast some weeks before the first scheduled transcontinental train, and returning to the mountains to spend the summer painting. Hindered by the smoke of forest fires in the Selkirks, he seems to have spent most of his time in the Rockies. On returning east he stopped off in Montreal, perhaps to meet with Van Horne, before going on to Boston, where he was living, to complete the black-and-white sketches for the vice-president's approval. Van Horne did not approve and requested specific changes in a letter to Fraser:

The black and white sketches will hardly answer our purposes, the mountain not being sufficiently imposing. I made last night a rough sketch in lamp-black which will illustrate my ideas: it is made mostly from memory and I have taken a great deal of license but I do not think that any one going to the spot without the picture in hand will ever accuse us of exaggeration. For the great glacier and Syndicate Peak I would like something similar to this. Since the thing has got cold I find the perspective in the glacier not right and the peaks projecting through the glacier are not treated broadly enough to give their proper distance. You will of course be able to make a great many improvements on my sketch, but I hope you will preserve the size.

Please make a sketch of Mount Stephen, treating it in something the same manner.

Clearly Van Horne was not above exaggeration for effect in material produced for tourist consumption, something that was equally obvious in many of the claims made in the company's "Swiss" campaign. But the "license" he took in this exaggeration was nothing in comparison with the affront to an artist of Fraser's stature in telling him how to do his work. Van Horne should have realized this as an artist himself, but he was more a railway general than an artist, used to having those who worked for him obey his every command without question, and apparently never thought twice about his action. As for Fraser, he was undoubtedly taken aback by the presumptuousness of the suggested changes but because of his basic insecurities and his financial needs, as the father of a large family, he realized Van Horne's power to help or hinder his career and decided to acquiesce rather than fight. In his reply he stated "I think your idea is far better than mine," and when the work was completed in late December he sent it with a letter that in part read "I

Fraser's black and white sketch of Mount Stephen, later rendered into an engraving, was radically altered at Van Horne's insistence

hope it will better realize your ideal [but] if it does not it is certainly not for want of trying for I have done all that I know." The requested sketch of Mount Stephen was similarly treated by Van Horne and to this Fraser's response was "your composition for Mt. Stephen is first rate." On completing this piece Fraser signed it and sent it off to Van Horne, and then, on thinking it over, wrote the following, making the ultimate bow in the vice-president's direction:

I fear that in my anxiety to get away the Mt Stephen I mechanically & without due thought signed it with my name.

If so it was a mistake as whatever credit is due to you alone. I have merely interpreted your idea for the engraver and would wish you to instruct him if it is not too late to make any alteration in that respect that you choose and upon consideration I think that the same holds true in the matter of the Glacier.

Van Horne appears to have taken Fraser at his word, for two engravings that fit the description of those discussed appeared in *The New Highway to the East* under the titles "Mount Stephen, Near The Summit Of The Rockies" and "The Heart Of The Selkirks, View Near Glacier House" without Fraser's signature. A third, "Beaverfoot Range, Rocky Mountains, Near Leanchoil Station, B.C.," which was probably the one referred to originally done for *The Century Magazine* from O.B. Buell's photograph, was signed by Fraser in the original edition of the pamphlet. However, when it was later used in a revised edition of the pamphlet, entitled *The New Highway to the Orient*, with the corrected caption "Ottertail Range, Rocky Mountains, Near Leanchoil Station, B.C.," Fraser's signature was very pointedly scratched out.

Although he appears to have been the only artist actually commissioned by the company in these years, Fraser was not the only one to benefit from its assistance. In 1886 several of his brother artists from Toronto and Montreal were in the west, in their cases the extent of CPR largesse having been free transportation. Because of growing requests for such privileges, Van Horne had to strike a policy quickly, perhaps first stating it in a letter to the Rev. Thomas Sommerville of Glasgow in June, 1885:

We are receiving a great number of applications of a similar nature from literary men, artists etc.; so many indeed that it has been found necessary to follow a definite and consistent line of conduct in them all. In such cases where a pass is applied for as you have done we inform the applicant that before we can say whether we will carry him free, we must have the opportunity not only of judging his work, but also of the channel through which it will reach the public. If then we are satisfied that the Company are likely to benefit by the venture and that the magazine or journal in which the paper or article is published is of sufficiently good standing to ensure its favourable reception and command respect we will be happy to refund to the traveller all the fare he may have paid on our railway.

While this was probably the official line it was not strictly adhered to in the case of artists belonging to the RCA or,

indeed, to some artists with international reputations from outside Canada. Most often passes were granted to artists on the recommendation of fellow artists who had previously received a pass or on the approval of well-known people interceding with Van Horne on their behalf. For example, in 1886 Lucius O'Brien used his acquaintance with Sir Charles Tupper, Canadian High Commissioner in London, to ask him to solicit from Van Horne travel privileges to the mountains and British Columbia so that he could execute some works for a forthcoming London exhibition. Tupper was successful in convincing Van Horne, and O'Brien spent a profitable summer, the first of several, sketching and painting along the line. Van Horne was pleased with the results and the following year O'Brien not only requested a pass for himself but also passes for his colleagues Thomas Mower Martin, Forshaw Day and Marmaduke Matthews. Thereafter these artists and others who received their first pass in the same manner wrote personally to Van Horne to seek their renewal.

The passes the artists liked were those with layover privileges so that they could stop and work for as long as they liked wherever they fancied. It appears that it was entirely up to Van Horne's whim if this or the normal pass without stopovers was to be granted. Some artists asked for more but were rarely granted it. F.M. Bell-Smith, another popular watercolourist of the day, requested in 1888 that a private car be put at his disposal in return for some mountain paintings, but a reply from Van Horne's secretary warned him not to ask for too much. In a further missive to the secretary, Bell-Smith writes "Thank you for the advice, I will be most cautious," and at the top of the letter it was noted that passes were sent to him a short time later. Apparently the only artist ever to be allowed a private car was the famous western American landscape painter Albert Bierstadt, who in 1889 was invited to make his pilgrimage to the mountains with all the resources the CPR could muster at his disposal.

What the CPR gained in return for these passes varied with the individual case. In many instances the artist attempted to sell his work to the railway but works were rarely bought by the company directly. Sometimes Van Horne or other company officials bought a painting, as in the case of Stephen's purchase of the three Fraser paintings, and even more frequently they were given a painting by an artist grateful for courtesies extended to him. In January, 1888, Lucius O'Brien presented Van Horne with a sketch of the Kicking Horse Pass; in November, 1889, Marmaduke Matthews asked him to select any painting from his summer's work then on exhibit at the Toronto Art Gallery; and in May, 1890, Albert Bierstadt made a gift of his painting "Sunrise from Glacier Station" to George Stephen because the artist "felt under some obligation to him for his repeated invitations to go westward."

The fact that these works usually ended up in the private collections of CPR officials did not preclude their use in promotional material. Likewise, engravings and photographic reproductions were used widely in illustrating the popular journals of the day, including *The Illustrated London News* and *The Graphic* in Britain, *Harper's Weekly* and *Frank Leslie's Illustrated Newspaper* in the United States and *The Dominion Illustrated* in Canada, giving these images and information on the CPR a huge distribution. For example, the front page of *The Illustrated London News* of July 24, 1886, less than a month after the beginning of transcontinental service, carried reproductions of four Notman photographs under the headline "The Canadian Pacific Railway." The exhibitions of the RCA also brought many pieces painted by artists on railway passes to Canadian public view, and most of the artists mentioned tried to have an annual exhibition in London as well as periodic showings in New York or other American cities, thereby bringing them to the attention of an international audience of potential tourists. Similarly, the CPR participated in many of the international expositions of the period and often used paintings as a focal point of their displays.

A case in point was the commission by Stephen of the three works by Fraser for display at the Colonial and Indian Exhibition held in London in 1886, a preview of Queen Victoria's Golden Jubilee in 1887. Because Fraser finished them too late to be sent to England by normal transportation, Van Horne had them taken over and hand-delivered to Alexander Begg. He in turn "arranged with Sir Charles Tupper as soon as they arrived to have them properly hung in one of the best positions in the Canadian Art Gallery." Unfortunately when Begg went down to examine how the pictures were placed he found them in positions "which were neither prominent nor befitting the character of the pictures themselves." After representations were made to Tupper, the

BRIDGE OVER THE COLUMBIA RIVER.

RAILWAY OVER THE PLAINS AT CALGARRY.

THE SURPRISE CREEK BRIDGE SELKIRK MOUNTAINS.

MOUNT STEPHEN SUMMIT OF THE ROCKY MOUNTAINS.

matter was satisfactorily settled, for Begg reported that "so far as Fraser's pictures are concerned they occupy a good position in the Gallery, better, I think, almost than those of O'Brien. For this Fraser has to thank in large measure the fact that three of his works have been painted for the President."

The Fraser paintings were viewed by thousands of Britons who could consider the wonders of the landscape that the line would open up with the first transcontinental train a few weeks later. The CPR also used the large reception room at its Cannon Street office in London as a gallery for Canadian landscape paintings and some of the paintings were circulated around England, largely in emigration promotion, to hotels, reading

The 1886 Colonial and Indian Exhibition in London provided the opportunity for potential British tourists to view impressive displays and the paintings of artists such as Fraser and O'Brien

rooms and agricultural fairs. Photographs by Notman, Buell, Henderson and others received an even wider distribution and often appeared in the display windows of the London office and in the windows of other agencies. Even more importantly they were supplied to travelling lecturers, who, like Buell himself, through the use of the recently invented lantern slide projector, were able to make them available to audiences of potential settlers or tourists in out-of-the-way places.

To return to the photographers, some of William McFarlane Notman's 1884 pictures had been used in preparing the reproductions for a section of twenty-two scenes in British Columbia for the last segment of *Picturesque Canada*. These had been valuable in providing the Canadian public, and potential tourists, with one of their first views of the country that the CPR was about to open up. Because of this success and the extensive use of Notman material in promotional literature, William McFarlane and his brother Charles returned to the

west in 1887, provided with Car No. 1, a photographer's car complete with darkroom fitted up for Professor Buell the year before. Some of their time was spent adding to the 1884 collection of mountain views, but they also continued through to Victoria, photographing as they went along. In 1889 the two repeated their visit, again provided with a photographic car for their private use. On both occasions the Notmans took some views with large-format "mammoth plate" cameras, emulating the work of western American photographers such as W.H. Jackson. As for Henderson, he did not return to the west until 1892 and may possibly have made another trip in 1897. By the time of the 1892 trip he had reached an agreement with David McNicoll to act as company photographer, spending at least four months in the field every year. Buell also seems to have travelled over the line on several other occasions and he too later claimed to have held "a commission as official photographer." The establishment of this position indicates the company's dedication to the photographic medium and was probably related to its entry into the commercial end of the business. An advertisement in one of the 1892 brochures read: "The Company now have on sale in their hotels, principal ticket offices, and on the trains, several series of handsomely finished views of scenes along their line of railway. Size: 12 by 10 inches, in portfolios suitable for the table (12 views in each series), Price $1.50: and views 22 by 28 inches, suitable for framing (3 views in a set), in mailing tube, Price $1.00" The portfolio sets were called *Glimpses Along The Canadian Pacific Railway* with subtitles such as *Mountain Series A* or *Indian Series A*, depending on the subject matter, and contained numerous Notman views as well as others, some possibly the work of Buell and Henderson.

Clearly the management of the CPR, and Van Horne in particular, played a key role in the support of artistic endeavour, be it photographic, painting or drawing, during the early years of the company's transcontinental history. It is equally clear that the demands of the CPR's advertising campaign influenced the subject matter of these endeavours. While it is likely that artists and photographers would naturally have gravitated to the mountains, it is questionable if they would have given them such painstaking attention were it not for the company's needs. A Toronto newspaper, *The Globe*, commenting on the joint RCA-OSA exhibition held in that city in 1888, criticized the preponderance of mountain material exhibited, although at the same time it recognized the importance of the CPR-inspired movement to both the country and Canadian art:

This…collection is one of the strongest exhibitions of Canadian work yet seen in the Queen City. It augurs well for Canadian art, and is especially strong in water color landscape…. The result of focusing so much attention on the beauties of Canadian scenery cannot but have a salutary effect on both home and foreign markets — to put it commercially; to encourage native painters, enabling young Canada to form a school of her own that shall not be ashamed to compete with the older civilisations. The only drawback at this juncture is that perhaps there is somewhat too much Rocky Mountain. Excellent as most of it is, it wants scattering by purchase.

Boosting Canada and its artists, the CPR achieved a reputation as a patron of the arts and guaranteed its supply of high-quality illustrative material to attract tourists. That the latter objective

was the more important of the two there can be no doubt. Perhaps the CPR's philosophy on the matter was best summed up in a letter from Van Horne to Archer Baker in 1889 concerning some Notman photographs, probably mammoth plates, to be displayed at the forthcoming Paris Exhibition:

I presume you will have the opportunity to see the pictures in question if you have not done so already. They are very effective in themselves but I would like to hear from you whether you think they can be used effectively on your side of the Atlantic. They are of course too expensive to put in any but the most public places. Is there a place in London where they could all be shown at once for a considerable time where everybody would see them? I mean everybody of the class that travels?

One of the popular destinations of Cook's tourists was Switzerland where they could enjoy the scenery as well as healthy outdoor pursuits, factors seized on by the CPR in its own "Canadian Alps" advertising campaign

IV: The Class That Travels

To understand the appeal of the CPR's promotional campaign for tourists in the years immediately after the inauguration of transcontinental service, it is necessary to be aware of some of the trends in Victorian travel. Beginning in the middle of the nineteenth century a revolution had begun in British travel that was to strongly influence the type of people the CPR would eventually attract. This revolution was the successor to a more important movement, the Industrial Revolution, which profoundly affected the English social system, resulting in the upward mobility of much of the working class into a new middle class. In the midst of this social process, Thomas Cook, head of the South Midlands Temperance Association, had begun excursions for the working classes to the English countryside and seaside as part of his commitment to the Temperance Movement and the bettering of the lot of the working man. Cook soon moved into travel as a business, developing Continental tours for the new middle class in the 1860s. Once these tours became established and Cook's scheme gained an air of respectability, the upper middle class and even the gentry began expressing an interest and eventually took part in more elaborate excursions as far afield as Egypt in the 1870s. In 1872, the year Jules Verne wrote his futuristic *Around the World in Eighty Days*, Cook offered his first round-the-world excursion.

These developments in tourism were taking place against the background of the growing strength and size of the British Empire. As a result, those travelling were usually imbued with the convictions of British supremacy. As Edmund Swinglehurst, the author of *The Romantic Journey*, a history of Thomas Cook and English Victorian travel, put it:

Under the circumstances it is not surprising that British tourists went abroad with the air of landlords inspecting their property, and they went in ever increasing numbers. Half a million at the beginning of the 1890s had turned to a million by the turn of the century. These tourists were no longer driven by a thirst for knowledge, nor were they prepared to put up with inconveniences. They wanted and expected to find themselves treated in a manner suitable to an Englishman's station in the world, to be provided with a decent, comfortable room and board, deferential service, and the English newspapers at breakfast.

In its advertising campaign, with its hints of English snobbery and emphasis on comfort and convenience, the CPR showed a remarkable (and profitable) understanding of this Imperial tourist market.

Also emerging in the second half of the nineteenth century was a new awareness and appreciation of wilderness and the beauty of nature. Prior to this time the history of mankind had been an almost continuous story of attempting to conquer and subjugate wilderness and nature so that it could be exploited for man's purposes. That this attitude should begin to change was nothing short of revolutionary, and again it too at least partly had its roots in the Industrial Revolution. Only when freed from concerns about maintaining the basics of life can man truly indulge in cultivating the mind and considering his relationship to the world. Therefore, the same Industrial Revolution that provided the money and the leisure time to enable the middle classes to travel also helped to provide the milieu in which man could re-assess the world to be travelled in. Hints of changing attitudes towards nature had been present from the time of the nature-poetry of the English Romantics through the early nineteenth-century writings of such American authors as James Fenimore Cooper and Washington Irving, who found inspiration in the wilderness for their work. However, the concept of the wilderness received its classical expression at the hands of another American author, Henry D. Thoreau, whose seminal *Walden* was published in 1854. According to Thoreau "in wilderness is the preservation of the world," a thought picked up by other authors, including John Muir, who made the somewhat similar statement "in God's wilderness lies the hope of the world." Quickly the idea of the value of undisturbed nature for its own sake and the equivalent desire to study it and participate in its recreational possibilities swept the United States and spread overseas. The most obvious concrete result of the movement was the creation in 1872 of Yellowstone National Park to preserve for the public such natural wonders as geysers, hot springs, canyons and mountains.

Summer Tours 1894 By the Canadian Pacific Railway.

Great Glacier of the Selkirks

The western focus of the CPR's tourist campaign and the dedication of the railway artists must be considered in the light of this movement. John Ruskin, the foremost British arbiter on all things good and beautiful, stated that "mountains are the beginning and the end of natural landscape," and as the epitome of wilderness and awesome natural beauty it was inevitable that they should become the most important aspect of that focus. It was interesting that the first and some of the most successful of Thomas Cook's Continental tours in the 1860s had been to Switzerland, where the excursionists had been inspired by the scenery and by the healthy outdoor activities they participated in, such as scrambling in the Alps. Great Britain had no public wilderness left at home and the possibility of experiencing it in the undeveloped parts of the Empire was attractive.

Thus all the elements that would appeal to the British tourist were to be found in the Canadian west — the British Empire expanding to open up the frontier, communion with nature in the wilderness, grand alpine scenery combined with the possibility of rugged physical challenge, and opportunity to fish and hunt to one's content. At the same time, because of the passion of the British for travel, the Continent had become extremely crowded and the idea of a virtually uninhabited western wilderness was enticing to many who had recently been jammed in a Swiss inn with too many fellow travellers. Van Horne was aware that all these influences were at work and played upon them like a virtuoso in his English campaign.

Van Horne was also aware that Canadians, with their close British connection, would be attracted to travel in their own country by the same advertising campaign that was primarily aimed at Great Britain. Attracting the American tourist was a different matter. There was a ready tourist market in the eastern United States where a fairly wealthy, optimistic and inquisitive population were eager to see the wonders and the wilderness of the North American continent. Several American transcontinental lines competed for their patronage, and Van Horne realized that to gain American tourists, the CPR had to offer a more attractive trip or persuade them to travel partly in the United States and partly in Canada. Either way American travel in Canada depended very heavily on the connections available between the CPR and American lines, and this in part accounts for the heavy emphasis Van Horne put on securing these connections in the years immediately after the completion of the CPR's route to the Pacific.

One of the most important of these American connections was the Minneapolis, St. Paul & Sault Ste. Marie Railway, known as the Soo Line, which provided access between St. Paul, Minnesota, and Sault Ste. Marie, Ontario, and ultimately the CPR main line at Sudbury. The CPR acquired an interest in the line in 1888, followed by control through majority stock ownership in 1890. In 1893 a branch from this line by way of Portal, North Dakota, tied in with a CPR branch line, built at the same time, to link with Moose Jaw, Saskatchewan. Another important line which the CPR also acquired control of in 1890 was the Duluth, South Shore and Atlantic Railway, running along the south shore of Lake Superior from the "Soo" to Duluth. A third was a line built to Windsor in 1889 which, by agreement with the Wabash Railway, provided access to Detroit and Chicago. And lastly, in 1889, the company acquired a true transcontinental status with the completion of the "Short Line" linking Montreal with Mattawamkeag, Maine. From this point, lines of the Maine Central and New Brunswick railway systems enabled the CPR to reach Saint John, N.B.

A pamphlet entitled *Summer Tours By The Canadian Pacific Railway* was developed specifically for the North American market and began appearing about 1888. It went through constant revisions as new lines were added and more country of interest to the tourist was opened up. In format *Summer Tours* was broken up into sections, "Eastern Tours," "Western Tours" and "Miscellaneous Tours." By 1891 the eastern section included such tours as "The New Short Line to the Maritime Provinces," "To Lower St. Lawrence and Gulf Ports" and "To Mount Desert and the Maine Coast;" the miscellaneous section included "To the Thousand Islands and down the St. Lawrence River," "To Niagara Falls, Buffalo and Chautauqua Lake;" and the western section included "Across the Continent, via the C.P. Rwy. Transcontinental Route," "To the West, via Sault Ste. Marie and Rail" and "To the North-west, via Chicago and St. Paul." Also in the western section was information on connections that could be made on the Pacific coast between San Francisco or Seattle and Vancouver, either overland or by steamship.

This west coast connection was the key to the company's

Thunder Cape

Kakabeka Falls

Red Rock, Nepigon Bay

Gorge Below Kakabeka Falls

A BIT OF JOE'S POINT ON THE ST. CROIX ST. ANDREWS N.B.

attempts to convince Americans travelling across the continent on a U.S. line in one direction that they should travel the other direction on the CPR. The program was fairly successful and many American tourists followed this route, travelling on one of the American transcontinentals, the Union Pacific or the Northern Pacific, taking a steamer up the coast to Victoria or Vancouver, perhaps going on a cruise to Alaska, and then returning home by way of the Canadian Pacific and one of the connecting lines. The comments of one tourist, Charles Rebstock of St. Louis, Missouri, made in the late 1890s at Glacier House sum up a trip of this type:

No two months tour in any part of the world equals the one which I finish in a few days.

The journey commences at Buffalo through the great lakes to Duluth, on the magnificent S. S. "Northwest", by rail through the world renowned wheat fields of Dakota and Minnesota, a week in the Wonderland "The Yellowstone Park" in coaches of perfect construction & most excellent equipment, a sail of 11 days, in the good S. S. "City of Seattle", along the coast of Alaska with its hundreds of pine covered islands, its snow capped mountains & glaciers, and lastly, but not least, the imcomparable trip through the Rocky Mountains on the Canadian Pacific R. R., here can be seen the most majestic and grandest scenery in any land reached by the iron horse — Indeed, I can say, "Eureka" (I have found it), the gem of all my travel in 4 continents.

The proportion of tourists from various countries travelling on the CPR in its first years of transcontinental operation is somewhat difficult to determine. Dean Carmichael noted that it was a very cosmopolitan group:

One day a gentleman gave us a long description of the railway system in India and of the license laws in New Zealand. We had descriptions of Bismarck, the deceased Emperors, the present Emperor and Von Moltke from a German gentleman who might well have passed himself off as Bismarck's brother. We had chats about sleighing in Northern Russia, about sunsets in Norway, and bush life in Australia, and one would fancy that England, France, Germany, Japan and China were stations on the road, one heard so much about them. A straw shows how the wind blows, and no one could ask for clearer evidence of the way in which the C.P.R. has brought Canada in touch with the most widely separated parts of the world than the cosmopolitan talk that a silent man can listen to in the well-cushioned smoking-room of a C.P.R. parlor car.

A more meaningful indicator is an analysis of the guests registered at the company's premier tourist resort, the Banff Springs Hotel. During its first season, June to October, 1888, the Banff Springs had a total of 1,503 guests; of these 801 or 53% were from Canada, 389 or 26% from the United States, 289 or 19% from Great Britain and 24 or 2% from other countries. From 1888 the number of tourists rose steadily, reaching a peak of 3,389 in 1891. Interestingly, the proportion of British and other-country guests changed very little, 494 or 15% and 147 or 4% respectively. However a complete reversal in the American and Canadian statistics had taken place by 1891 with 861 or 25% of the guests being Canadian and 1,887 or 56% being American. Thereafter the statistics began to tumble, graphically recording the effects of a worldwide economic depression. By 1893 the number of guests had declined to 2,325, a drop attributed to the economic situation, bad weather and the Chicago World's Fair, to which the CPR ran special excursions. But except in the category of other countries, where the proportion rose to 10% representing 25 countries, the percentages remained relatively static, undoubtedly giving management food for thought in the amount of time and money devoted to British promotion compared to the obviously more successful American promotion.

Fortunately, it is possible to ascertain just *who* some of these tourists were, as the 1890s may be accurately described as the golden age of the tourist travel account. Seemingly, it was *de rigueur* for any tourist who was anyone to publish an account of his or her journey in the home newspaper or journal. Those who could afford it or could attract the eye of a publisher might also have their stories appear in book form. Actually those who had their accounts published formed only a small proportion of the tourists travelling the line, but it is interesting to examine

The Chicago World's Fair, at which the CPR had a display, was promoted as a destination for tourist excursions, contributing to a decline in Canadian Rockies tourism in 1893. G. O. Abnold photograph

some of their reactions and impressions since they were undoubtedly typical.

The Canadian quartet of travellers featured in the privately-circulated *A Holiday Trip* were from what would have to be considered the upper class of Canadian society. Like others of that class they saw in the opening of the Canadian west not only an economic hinterland for the east but also the opportunity for Canada to achieve its true greatness. Their spokesman, Dean Carmichael, saw the first transcontinental train leaving Montreal and "as he joined his voice in a speeding cheer, he realized that Canada was at last developing — and that boldly and bravely — a new-born faith in its own destiny as an important factor in the enterprise and trade of the world." Understandably, his account concentrated only on the positive aspects of transcontinental travel. However, travellers from

other parts of the world did not necessarily have the same vested interest in promoting the Dominion and, in some cases, gave what was perhaps a more accurate description of such a trip. In this vein the account of Edward Roper entitled *By Track and Trail, A Journey Through Canada*, illustrated with the author's own sketches and published in 1891, is of interest. Roper was a gentleman of independent means from Kent, a Fellow of the Royal Geographical Society and an experienced traveller, having visited Australia, New Zealand and Canada previous to the 1887 trip recorded in his book.

Several things that Roper mentioned in his account are of interest in the picture of Canadian tourism at the time. There was a strong relationship in Britain between emigration and tourist promotion, and Roper witnessed the relative success of the campaigns when speaking to fellow passengers aboard a ship bound for Canada: "I know quite well with what object a number of my fellow voyagers are bound to Canada: some few for pleasure, certainly, but nine hundred out of the thousand on board are going 'to better themselves,' at any rate they hope so." One of the passengers with whom he became particularly friendly, a Mr. Selby, was a good example of the tourist-emigration crossover that often occurred.

A widower somewhat over fifty, Selby had decided to spend £400 to take his family of two daughters and one son to Canada to see the country and determine if it was wise to settle there, or, as he put it, to "look before I leap." In conversations with Roper he gave some idea of his thoughts on railway and other advertising. His son "was enthusiastic, and would long since have had me sell my property at home, and write out to Canada to buy land and have a house built ready for us. If I had done that, we should now be going to settle in the Great North-West, without knowing more about it than steamship and railroad companies publish in their pamphlets, and land agents advertise for our information."

Roper concurred: "True enough, admitting that most of what we read in such publications is true, there is much equally true which is not found in them, and which only hard experience can teach."

Van Horne would have been pleased with the initial comments Roper made about the CPR after boarding it at Quebec. Roper found the system of checking baggage through to be "a blessing;" he commented on the punctuality of the trains; he stated that "nothing can be more luxurious than the sleeping cars of the C.P.R.;" and he found that "the coloured attendant, or porter, was polite — very different to former experiences of mine on American railroads." He also mentioned a facet of CPR travel that had not been a part of the railway's advertising campaign but which Van Horne would undoubtedly have liked — its sociability: "Then we had to make acquaintance with our fellow passengers, for travelling in this way is much more a social affair than in our way of going about by rail at home. It is, indeed, very much like being at sea." On approaching the Rocky Mountains he imparted the feeling of growing anticipation that the CPR's own literature tried to give: "We were a merry party in the car that evening. The little excitement at Gleichen had stirred us all up, and we were full of anticipation; for to-morrow morning, if all went

well, we should have left the plains and be amongst the Rocky Mountains, and then, we were assured, there would not be a moment day or night but would be full of interest and excitement."

In the CPR literature the mountains were the glorious climax to which the narrative built; in Roper's they became a challenge to survive with his skin intact. The weather brought heavy snow, the rivers rose and one of the bridges near Banff was nearly washed out. After waiting several hours in the blizzard, Roper's party, which included the Selby family, were forced to cross the weakened bridge on foot, on slippery ties in the teeth of the blowing snow. Once over safely they waited what seemed an interminable time until a train from the west came to pick them up. They were then unceremoniously herded into a common coach with all the other passengers instead of being provided with the sleeping car their tickets guaranteed.

The conductor promised "that at Banff, a few stations ahead, we should get a sleeper, a diner and every C.P.R. luxury," but when they arrived after dark there was no transportation available to the hotel, and nothing to eat but cheese and crackers. Continuing their trip in the coach, they proceeded to the Kicking Horse Pass, where the air brakes were suddenly applied and everyone was thrown out of their seats just as "a stone as big as a man's head came crashing through the window of the car, fortunately without hurting anyone." This was followed by the terrible sounds of rock pouring down the mountainside and striking the side of the car, miraculously not knocking it off the track and into the abyss. It took several hours for a crew to dig out the train. Then, past Field, it ran into dark clouds of smoke from a forest fire and "everything was black and scorched. The telegraph poles were in flames here and there, and the bridges we crossed were only saved from destruction by the utmost exertions of the 'section men' who are stationed in gangs along the line to protect them." The train had to move slowly so that each bridge could be inspected before it was crossed and was again halted altogether because a burning tree had fallen across a bridge in front of it. Another delay of several hours was required to remove the obstruction before the train could proceed to Donald, where the oft-promised sleeping car was nowhere to be found. The train was again stopped by a tremendous snowslide just beyond the Loop, and the Roper group were settling in for another night in the coach when the conductor visited the car, announcing "in a loud and cheery voice, 'By the Company's orders, and at their expense, all "sleepers" are to take up their quarters at the Glacier House until the road is clear.'"

As it turned out, Roper and his party had to spend two nights, albeit comfortable ones, at Glacier House before the line was cleared. Then, upon continuing, they were delayed again near Revelstoke for a long period, although they were now comfortable in a first-class sleeper and "the Company, regretting our delay, had ordered dinner for all the passengers." The rest of the trip went off without a hitch. Several days behind schedule, the train reached Vancouver where Roper was greeted by "one of the tip-top C.P.R. officials, whom I knew.... 'On time you see. I told you in Montreal our trains were always on time. They *always* arrive here at 12.50, after nearly a three thousand mile trip.'"

Roper's account pointed out in great detail some of the realities of a transcontinental rail trip at the time, belying the

As Roper's account pointed out, delays were frequent in the mountains, leaving passengers to pass the time as best they could

CPR's promise in *The New Highway to the East* that "there will be no hardships to endure, no difficulties to overcome, and no dangers or annoyances whatever." Although few travellers experienced the amount of travail that he did, there was almost always some delay for one reason or another, a not unexpected occurrence given the type of wilderness the line traversed.

In leaving Roper's account it is interesting to note the fate of the Selby family, whose trials and tribulations are dealt with at great length in his book. Selby's son, Tom, and one of his daughters remained in Canada, settling at the prairie town of Broadview in what would become the province of Saskat-

A sociable gathering on the rear platform of Roper's sleeping car

chewan. Selby and his other daughter returned to England, unconvinced that they would be happy breaking their English ties for a life in the new land. The family's experiences were probably fairly typical, for there were many instances of tourists looking over the lay of the land before deciding whether or not to emigrate.

As for Roper, he returned to England by the steamship that had brought him out, and upon reaching home ended his narrative on a fairly positive note vis-a-vis the CPR: "There were tourists, some from 'round the world' getting home again. You heard Vancouver, Glacier House, Victoria, Yokohama, Melbourne, Sydney, and fifty other places, spoken of on deck or at table as familiarly as we speak of Charing Cross or Piccadilly at home; and nearly all were delighted with the new Canadian route, and with the C.P.R. arrangements...."

Another tourist account at least mildly critical of the CPR was *On The Cars And Off* by Douglas Sladen, published in 1895. A writer of some note, having published nine previous books and being a regular contributor to the journal *Queen* (in which some chapters of his book had appeared), Sladen was a prime example of the English tourist convinced of his superiority and expecting deference from all with whom he came in contact. Unlike Roper's, his barbs were not aimed at the CPR because of harrowing experiences and late schedules but rather because of dissatisfaction with other matters on which the company prided itself, service and comfort. Two particular objects of his ire were the conductor and the porter:

Like Japan and ancient Sparta, the cars are subject to a species of "dual monarchy," the parallel potentates being the conductor — who generally retires with a fortune acquired nobody know how, for he doesn't get tipped — and the negro porter. You might almost imagine the conductor was the captain of the ship, you see him so seldom, and he is so superior when he thrusts himself on your attention. The real autocrat of the sleeping car is, however, the negro, apparently selected for the lightness of his colour; for other qualifications are rare. There is one to each sleeper, and he talks of his ladies, and makes himself generally objectionable until the last day when he takes up most of your morning brushing you and other genial patronage. You give him a dollar, if you have not seen too much of him.

Other criticisms came in the matter of the comforts of CPR equipment, Sladen complaining that it was impossible to keep the ladies out of the smoking room of the parlour car and then, in the next breath, pointing out how difficult the sleeping car arrangements were for them:

...Sleeping cars test the stuff a woman is made of, perhaps I should say made up of. She cannot undress until she gets into her bunk, which, for getting out of her corsets and skirt, is about as convenient as her coffin, being hardly higher than the space between the shelves of a cupboard.

There is nowhere to pile up the multitudinous garments, hair, teeth, and so on, that she may shed, except the foot of her bunk, and she has to dress in the same commodious way in the morning. Under the circumstances, it is hardly surprising that the ladies who come on board looking the daintiest go off looking the worst....

In fairness to the CPR, Sladen mentioned that the problems with employees were endemic to all railways and that it actually measured up fairly well: "On the Canadian Pacific Railway they are pretty well behaved, because if there is one man in the world who stands no nonsense it is the President of the Canadian Pacific Railway." Similarly, its equipment was no worse than any other despite its discomforts, and on the whole he found travelling on the line "a pretty good sort of life." Nonetheless, Sladen's account, like Roper's, pointed up some of the realities of transcontinental rail travel in comparison with what the company's promotional material would have the potential tourist believe. Obviously CPR management felt that his criticisms were not unduly damaging and that as a popular author his work had some value, as *On The Cars And Off* was sold by newsagents on the trains for a time. This in itself was somewhat ironic in that Sladen had little good to say in his book about such "newsies": "Somewhere or other, under the coals of the tender, or upon the roof, there is a mysterious hoard from which the glib boy who walks up and down all day, like the fiend who tormented Job, produces inexhaustible supplies of

Glacier House, in its isolated mountain location, was frequently a refuge for CPR passengers forced to lay-over because of mishaps on the line. Notman photograph newspapers, pirated novels, fruits, candies (sweetmeats), tobacco, black silk caps, packs of cards, and anything else likely to cheer the victim of the railway...."

Fortunately for the company, most tourists' accounts tended to accentuate the positive, a fact not unrelated to the free passes and other courtesies many received from Van Horne. Perhaps the most blatant example of this was illustrated in the book *California And Alaska Over The Canadian Pacific Railway* by William Seward Webb, published in 1890. Webb was the epitome of eastern American money, an in-law of the Vanderbilts and the owner of his own custom railway car manufacturing company, the Wagner Palace Car Company. In 1889 he decided to take his family, a few relatives and some friends on a trip in a private train, composed of a baggage car, a dining car, and two special cars, across the United States to California, up to Canada, and then by steamer to Alaska. The train was to be run as a special, independent of any timetables, which would allow it to set its own speed and thereby relieve the party "of any anxiety they might otherwise have had in regard to making connections." The train was described by the author as "probably the most thoroughly equipped and luxurious one that has ever been used by a party of travellers."

The lengths to which Van Horne went to provide for Webb's party while they were in Canada were truly amazing. They travelled via St. Paul to Winnipeg, where their train hooked up to a CPR locomotive and immediately headed west, as "it was the wish of Mr. Van Horne that we should go directly through to the coast, and stop at different points on the Canadian Pacific road on our return." At each divisional point a new locomotive specifically designated for Webb's train stood fuelled and ready to go on his arrival. At Swift Current the party was joined by John Niblock, a subdivision superintendent in the Western Division, who was provided to give details and descriptions of the country passed through. At Donald, Niblock left the train and was replaced by his counterpart on the Mountain Subdivision, Richard Marpole, who performed the same service the rest of the way to the Pacific. On arriving at Vancouver they were greeted by Harry Abbott, general superintendent of the Pacific Division, who extended to them "the courtesies of the road at this terminus," including a buggy ride to explore the new Stanley Park, "which promises some day to be one of the wonders of the coast."

THE SPECIAL TRAIN

Webb's dalliance in Vancouver was necessary to await the arrival of the steamship *Islander*, which was to take his party on a cruise to Alaska, another perk the CPR helped to provide: "Through the kindness of Mr. Van Horne, of Montreal, a new steel steamship, belonging to the Canadian Pacific Steamship Company, and which, about this time, had just arrived on the Pacific coast, was chartered for a two weeks' cruise in Alaskan waters. She was entered as the writer's yacht in the Yacht Club, and carried his yachting colors during the cruise." Over the ten days the party was away cruising, Abbott had CPR crews go to work on the train and when Webb returned he was delighted to find all the cars had been overhauled and painted and "looked better now than the day we started from New York." Reboarding, the travellers started on their leisurely way east, stopping wherever their fancy took them. At Banff they stayed over at the Banff Springs Hotel and Webb paid it a high compliment for one as familiar with hotels as he obviously was, stating that "it was as good as any hotel we stopped at on our journey, almost equalling the hotel at Monterey."

Proceeding to Medicine Hat, the party was joined by Niblock's assistant, who was to provide them with some hunting at two noted refuges of waterfowl, Goose Lake and Rush Lake. There being no siding at the former spot, when they arrived there early in the morning the train simply stopped on the main line. The assistant then took out a telegraph set and sent off a message to halt all traffic through the area while the gentlemen took their sport. Later on, at Lake Nipigon east of Fort William, the travellers were similarly well treated when they desired to do some fishing. They found that the head of the Hudson's Bay Company in that district "had been notified by Mr. Van Horne to have everything ready for us in the way of necessary supplies; also canoes and Indians."

Shortly after completing their successful fishing trip, Webb and his party continued on to Montreal and then to Shelburne, Vermont, where their incredible journey ended. In closing off his narrative he gave Van Horne a ringing commendation for the hospitality and services he had provided:

Before closing this record of our western trip, it is only proper to say that the whole party were unanimous in the opinion that the courtesy and kind attention shown by Mr. Van Horne and all the officials connected with the Canadian Pacific Railway could never be fully repaid, and it was only through their efforts that our trip had been so thoroughly enjoyable and interesting. It is not too much to say that Mr. Van Horne literally verified the statement made in a letter to the writer prior to the commencement of our journey; that statement was that the Canadian Pacific Railway was at the disposal of the writer to come and go as he willed, and all that he had to do was command. Mr. Van Horne's generous hospitality was certainly thoroughly appreciated by every member of the party, and will never be forgotten by the writer.

It is likely that at some future date Van Horne collected on Webb's debt of gratitude because Webb could help the CPR in many ways. However, part of the debt was repaid with the book itself as it described the CPR, its services, its scenery, its hotels and its personnel with glowing praise. Webb was certainly not the only tourist Van Horne helped and in return had the company's reputation enhanced in a subsequent tourist account, although in most cases the assistance offered was far less than that provided to him. More typically a pass would be provided to those of some social standing or of some literary reputation and in some cases assistance was given in finding suitable illustrations for the publication. A good example was W.S. Caine's book *A Trip Round The World In 1887-88*, published in 1892. Caine, the member of Parliament for Barrow-in-Furness in Lancashire, received a pass to travel on the line as a courtesy to one of his position and on the understanding that he would write a series of letters about his adventures that would be sent home to be printed in the *Barrow News*. Later deciding that he would publish the letters as a

book, he wrote to Van Horne and requested some photographic views of the scenery along the route. Van Horne was away at the time but Arthur Piers forwarded a selection of 104 Notman views in March, 1888, and when the vice-president returned he wrote personally to Caine:

Returning from British Columbia yesterday I found your recent letters... Mr. Piers has already advised you that your photos were forwarded some weeks ago.

I will be happy to assist you in any way possible in your proposed publication. We can send you some blocks illustrating our sleeping, dining and Colonist cars which have not yet been used. Our blocks illustrating the scenery along the line have been used repeatedly in our advertising material and you would not, I presume, care for them for that reason. I will send you by next month a few photos which you may find useful.

Much of the material provided was used by an artist making engravings for the book and in return Caine was profuse in his praise for the company, stating that "none of the transcontinental railways of the United States can compare with the Canadian Pacific either for beauty of scenery or comfort in travel."

One aspect of these tourist accounts is the degree to which they were similar in terms of the things they chose to describe. Seemingly such accounts were written with one of the CPR's annotated timetables or pamphlets in hand, the author constantly paraphrasing the company's own descriptions of attractions on the line. Niagara Falls was, of course, one of the premier tourist attractions of Canada (and the United States) and although it was somewhat out of the way, requiring a steamer trip on Lake Ontario from Toronto, the CPR always provided information in company publications on how it could be reached. Once there, the tourist was informed that both sides of the falls were previously in the hands of speculators who charged admission to the best vantage points but that Canadian and American authorities had cleared them out and had created parks in their stead. Almost without fail tourist accounts would mention this fact as well as stories of the

The site of Selwyn's misadventure was recorded in an 1884 Notman photograph entitled "The Tunnel that collapsed in Kicking Horse Pass." William McFarlane Notman photograph

exploits of numerous daredevil artists going over the falls in various types of boats or walking tightropes strung above them. Out on the prairies it was the famous Bell Farm near Indian Head, Saskatchewan, that was treated in a similar manner. It was touted in CPR material as the largest farm in the world, encompassing a hundred square miles of arable land, and this fact was never missed in the accounts of tourists passing through its centre on the main line. Nor did they fail to provide other detailed information about it, including the story of the ploughmen making furrows four miles long, despite the fact that not one of them ever appears to have actually stopped to visit it.

The popularity of the group excursion, which Thomas Cook had developed to such an extent in Great Britain, also affected Canada to some degree. However, in the early years of CPR transcontinental service these excursion groups tended not to be organized by a tour company but rather connected with a

meeting of some professional group or organization. In fact, the first tourists ever to travel to western Canada by rail were of this type and their trip took place before the line was even completed. The group was composed of ninety-eight of the Empire's foremost scientists who had been in attendance at the meeting of the British Association for the Advancement of Science at Toronto in the autumn of 1884. Leading the party was the same Dr. Alfred Selwyn of the Geological Survey of Canada who had led a party including Sandford Fleming and two Notman employees into the Rockies in 1871. Accompanying them, at Van Horne's specific request, was Dr. John Macoun, the pioneer Canadian naturalist, whose reports on the Canadian west had played a major part in the CPR's choice of route across the southern prairies and through the Rockies via the Kicking Horse Pass. Macoun, who later wrote his memories of the trip as a part of his autobiography, reported that the group had been able to get as far as the summit of the pass on the train before breaking up into smaller parties to do some exploring. Selwyn, leading the geological party, had made for a nearby tunnel "and was nearly killed by hammering on the rock at the mouth of the tunnel, which caused a fall of rock which blocked up the entrance, and no further progress in that direction could be made." As for Macoun, he and another botanist had taken the opportunity to climb the flanks of Cathedral Mountain "as far as my shoes would allow" and gained some beautiful views. Since the excursion party was accompanied by an artist for *The Graphic* and encountered a writer for *Collier's Magazine* it received a good deal of press coverage. Upon completion of the line, other excursions of a similar nature quickly followed, the largest being that of the Canadian Medical Association in 1889. Almost two hundred medical men were part of the group and an English Presbyterian minister who met them at the Banff Springs Hotel reported that "we heard no difference of opinion as to the unrivalled beauty and interest of the place."

Van Horne was often approached with propositions for the railway to provide free transportation for excursions of journalists, the idea being that their reports would provide the CPR with a multitude of publicity. He was rather sceptical of their value, an opinion illustrated in a letter replying to such a request from Nicholas Flood Davin, the newspaperman member of Parliament from Regina:

Replying to your note of the 18th inst., proposing a press excursion from the United Kingdom and Ireland. The utmost extent to which the Company would contribute to such an excursion would be free transportation over its own lines, and that only in case the party should be composed of bonafide and representative newspaper men which is frequently not the case with press excursions. An account of the excursion, of course, would be published in each of the newspapers represented, but I don't think it is ever read by any but the persons directly interested — those who went on the excursion or their families. You must pardon me, therefore, if I am not very enthusiastic about the excursion you suggest. Another reason for my lack of enthusiasm is that large excursion parties see very little, and what little they do see is seen too frequently in a bad light, for a large party is not easily provided for.

His lack of enthusiasm for excursions, journalistic or otherwise, was also partly due to their disruptive effect on regular traffic.

British tourists often went abroad with the air of landlords surveying their Empire

On one occasion in 1887 he severely criticized William Whyte, general superintendent of the Western Division, for making use of the reserve dining car between Winnipeg and Calgary for an excursion train:

…If an accident had happened to one of the other dining cars between Winnipeg and Calgary during the absence of the one in question, our regular trains would have been in a bad fix, and we will not for any excursion whatever interfere with the regular working of our through passenger trains…

I have notified the Passenger Department that we do not want any more excursions going more than one hundred and fifty miles that require special trains whether they pay or not, as we cannot handle them without re-arranging our business or taking some risk of doing so.

Our transcontinental passenger trains must be sacred and the cars belonging to them must not be disabled for any purpose whatever.

In spite of Van Horne's feelings about excursions, they remained an important part of the CPR's tourist business.

Apart from tourists' reactions to their trip across the country were their reactions to each other, an interesting social facet of CPR tourism in the early days of transcontinental service. The superior attitude with which the British travelled abroad has already been mentioned, but it is particularly interesting to note their attitude towards Americans and vice versa. Essentially the British tended to dislike Americans heartily, criticizing them for their "vulgarity" and loudness but secretly envying them for their wealth and easy self-assurance. For their part, the Americans found the British hard to stomach because of their feigned superiority, priggishness and lack of sense of humour. Between them stood the poor Canadian tourist, often regarded by the Americans as being too British and by the British as being too American. A few examples of these attitudes appeared in the tourist literature, but since it would have been beneath most writers' dignity to make too much of such things the criticisms usually took a very mild form. More direct were some of the entries made in a scrapbook established at Glacier House in the 1890s so that "the visitors to Glacier House should have the opportunity to enter their experiences of, and opinions on, the scenery within their reach; and thus to encourage others to enjoy the superb views too often passed by travellers in ignorance of their existence and of their accessibility to ordinary Tourists." Many took the opportunity to express their views on the scenery but others were more interested in expressing their opinions on fellow travellers.

One English tourist took it upon himself to instruct Americans and Canadians in the proper pronunciation of the word glacier: "I should like to point out to American & Canadian visitors to this place that the word Glacier is not pronounced Glazier as most of them think ("Glac" as in Lass). A glazier I may remind them is one who fixes window panes." Tit for tat, an American traveller soon afterwards made the following entry:

Although not particularly favoured by Van Horne, excursion parties, like this group at Glacier House, were an important element in CPR tourism. Trueman and Caple photograph

A fable for authors. Once upon a time an American Lady came to Glacier and not only visited the Glacier itself but also met a gentleman whom she called a Little Englander because the area of his mind was scarcely as big even as the little island he came from. Knowing his kind, she asked him with a spirit to be envied and with due solemnity whether the C.P.R. had put the Glacier there as an advertisement. Solemnly he treasured the sample of the intelligence of ladies from the States, and when with a friend he wrote his little book he solemnly printed the story on page 222. And the American lady has often told it all with glee to her American friends. Moral When Little Englanders travel here, they should be accompanied by some one from the "States" to point out to them what is a joke, and what is not a joke.

Despite the fact that there were several such skirmishes in the pages of the scrapbook there were also numerous very positive things said about the opportunity such a place provided for making friends and gaining an understanding of the country. One such entry, written by Frank G. Harris of Clearfield, Pennsylvania, perhaps more than any other succinctly and simply summed up the importance of tourism in helping foreigners to appreciate and gain an insight into Canada and Canadians:

I came here with my wife a few days ago intending to stop but one day. We are here yet, and I would like to stay longer. For years I have promised myself a trip across the Continent via the Canadian Pacific Railroad. I have seen most of the States, New Brunswick, and other Provinces but I take my hat off to Glacier and to these glorious old mountains. I like them most of all. I have enjoyed my trip across the Lakes, the Prairies and through these Canyons and Mountains. I go home with a better opinion of Canada and her people. There is no limit to the possibilities, to the future greatness of this Country, our good neighbours to the north. If I were not a Citizen of the U.S. I would be a Canadian…

From the humble beginnings of this crude "hotel" erected by railway workers at the Cave and Basin springs in 1883 sprang the CPR's world famous resort at Banff. "First structure at the Cave and Basin," J.D. Curren, n.d., oil on canvas, 51 x 61 cm.

v: Fifty Switzerlands in One

The CPR's tourist business ripened into a full-scale resort operation as its transcontinental passenger traffic increased in volume and sophistication. The Canadian Rockies ("our mountains" as Van Horne referred to them) became a holiday destination, not just the scenic high point of main-line travel, and the railway's Banff Springs Hotel, opened in 1888, was *the* place to stay. It offered all the comforts of the high-class English-speaking home (or French chateau, or European spa), and catered to every wilderness whim of the nineteenth-century tourist.

One of the main thrusts of CPR tourist policy was cooperation with the federal government in the development of national parks; Van Horne suggested their creation in 1883. Undoubtedly familiar with the Northern Pacific Railway's promotion of Yellowstone Park to attract tourists to its line, he had, on one of his first visits to the Rockies, recognized their park potential. An area that seemed appropriate was Lac des Arcs, a flood-plain enlargement of the Bow River just inside the Front Ranges along the CPR line, and he contacted William Pearce, Commissioner of Mines, suggesting it. The choice was an unfortunate one. Van Horne had seen the lake covered by a light dusting of snow in the late fall. In summer, exposed mudflats and frequent high winds made it an unlikely spot to create a tourist spa, and it was jokingly referred to by CPR workers as "Van Horne's Park" for a number of years afterwards. Recognizing his error, Van Horne did not pursue the matter, but neither did he drop the conviction that the idea of a park was a good one. When the federal government began to give consideration in 1885 to creating a reservation around the recently discovered hot springs on the slopes of Sulphur Mountain, the CPR gave its full support. During that summer Van Horne provided the means for some members of Parliament to travel over the new line to Banff. The same year the Deputy Minister of the Interior, A.M. Burgess, asked the CPR secretary, Charles Drinkwater, to submit suggestions for legislation. Drinkwater recommended that Canada follow the example of the reservation of Hot Springs, Arkansas, made in 1832 by the United States, and the Canadian government did just that, creating a reservation of approximately ten square miles around the springs in November, 1885. The following summer the CPR extended an invitation to members of both the Senate and the House of Commons to ride free over the new line to the Pacific coast and included a stopover at Banff with a visit to the Cave and Basin springs as part of the itinerary. The same year the Prime Minister, Sir John A. Macdonald, and his wife, Agnes, enjoyed a trip on the CPR and were much taken with the alpine scenery. By the time the legislation was introduced in Parliament in April, 1887, proposing to turn the Hot Springs Reservation into Canada's first national park, many of the politicians had become full-fledged boosters, including the Prime Minister, who enthused during the debate:

I do not suppose in any portion of the world there can be found a spot, taken altogether, which combines so many attractions and which promises in as great a degree not only large pecuniary advantage to the Dominion, but much prestige to the whole country by attracting the population, not only of this continent, but of Europe to this place. It has all the qualifications necessary to make it a great place of resort... There is beautiful scenery, there are the curative properties of the water, there is a genial climate, there is prairie sport and there is mountain sport; and I have no doubt that it will be a great watering place.

Macdonald regarded the park at Banff as the basis for establishing an international spa on the order of those at Baden-Baden and Bath where the wealthy would come and take the waters, attracting money and prestige to the Dominion. The idea of preserving the wilderness for its own sake was, as yet, somewhat in the future for the government of Canada. Similar ideals — money and prestige for the CPR — were also what motivated Van Horne. By the time the act creating the 260-square-mile Rocky Mountains Park (later Banff National Park) was given royal assent in late June, 1887, the CPR already had what was to be the new park's premier facility, the Banff Springs Hotel, well under construction.

The reservation at Banff in 1885 led to consideration of other park sites in the mountains. The member of Parliament for Lisgar in Manitoba, A.W. Ross, one of the foremost proponents of the park idea, expressed the opinion in the House and then later in a letter to the Minister of the Interior, Thomas White, that there should be reservations at Laggan (Lake Louise station), Mount Stephen, the summit of the Selkirks, Three Valley Lakes and Shuswap Lakes. A report by William Pearce supported these suggestions and recommended another at Albert Canyon. White sent copies of Ross's and Pearce's suggestions to Van Horne for comment, and he in turn asked for the opinions of some of his employees familiar with the mountains, particularly John Egan for those in the Western Division and Harry Abbott for those in the Pacific Division. Egan recommended reservations at the summit of the Rockies, around Mount Stephen and at Donald, and Abbott suggested areas around Mount Stephen, Mount Sir Donald and Eagle Pass. Van Horne, in a letter to White in June, 1886, concurred with Abbott's suggestions but added "I think that the amphitheatre at the Summit of the Selkirks [Rogers Pass] should be reserved as it is one of the most beautiful spots in the world." White agreed and in an order-in-council dated October 10, 1886, the areas suggested by Abbott, including the

Tourist photographing the Three Sisters near Canmore. Beatrise Longstaff Lance photograph

Within a few years the Cave and Basin had become one of the major tourist attractions developed by the federal government at Banff. Elliott Barnes photograph

amendment added by Van Horne in the Selkirks, became park reservations. Although the Eagle Pass reservation was later dropped as being unsuitable for park purposes, the other three became the nucleus of Yoho and Glacier National Parks.

Both the government and the railway realized that if the new parks were to become successful tourist areas, facilities and services would be necessary. And, since both had limited funds at their disposal, they should combine forces to provide these necessities. Generally speaking, the federal government provided the facilities, the Banff Springs Hotel being the exception, and the CPR provided the services.

Federal government surveyors laid out the Banff townsite adjacent to the Cave and Basin springs in the fall of 1886. At the same time the government began work on a series of roads linking the new town with its tourist attractions. Carriage roads to the Cave and Basin and to the Upper Hot Springs were laid out in 1886, to Lake Minnewanka in 1887, around the Loop at the base of Mount Rundle in 1889, to Sundance Canyon in 1892 and to the Hoodoos and the neighbouring town of Anthracite in 1893. The government upgraded both the Cave and Basin and the Upper Hot Springs, adding bathing and changing facilities; built an animal paddock and stocked it with buffalo, elk, sheep and such exotic animals as angora goats and yak; established a natural history museum; and provided a boat concession on the Bow River.

For its part, the CPR provided the means by which the tourist could visit these attractions as well as those to be found in the wilderness beyond the view of the parlour car. In 1893 it let a contract to provide the guests at the Banff Springs Hotel with safe, dependable transportation. The contractors were Colonel James Walker of Calgary, Major John Stewart of Ottawa and W.L. Mathews, manager of the hotel, who formed the CPR Transfer Company and built a substantial stable between the hotel and the town. This they stocked with a supply of three-seater, two-seater and democrat buggies to handle the demands of sightseers and with a few enclosed coaches to provide transportation for guests between the station and the hotel, a mile and a half distant. Douglas Sladen described these services and their popularity in *On The Cars and Off*:

> *Banff does, indeed, present the American cockney or invalid with the Rocky Mountains made easy. A very towny 'bus,' a much more luxurious affair than the Fifth Avenue stage, which caters for the smartest people in New York, conveys the passengers for the two miles from the station to the Banff*

> *Springs Hotel, which is nowhere near the Springs. You can hire a fly, for all the world like a Brighton fly, with a pair of horses, to drive you over excellent gravelled roads to the Devil's Lake, or to very near the top of the big mountain. The American cockney spends all day driving about in these flies, and all night long in buying ten-by-eight photographs.*

Such carriage drives were popular with tourists from all over the world, not just Americans, because they facilitated that most popular of all tourist activities, seeing the sights. Thousands each year visited the surrounding lakes and mountain viewpoints where they could "kodak" to their heart's content. Taking pictures with the revolutionary invention of George Eastman and its many imitators was becoming a mania with tourists throughout the country, no less a personage than Lady Aberdeen, wife of the Governor-General, writing a travel book in the early nineties entitled *Through Canada With A*

The CPR Transfer Company provided for the transportation needs of the guests at the Banff Springs Hotel. Boorne and May photograph

These tourists "kodaking" in the Fraser Canyon lent credence to Sladen's description of the mania for picture taking. Vaux family photograph

Kodak. Again it was Sladen, in his typical acerbic fashion, who best described the tourist's love affair with the camera:

The Canadian Pacific Railway ought to have a commission on detective cameras, Kodaks, hawkeyes, etc. for the average passenger would as soon think of going without antibilious medicines as without a camera. Whenever you stop at a station, all the steps getting down are packed with people taking pot shots with Kodaks. American children learn kodaking long before they learn how to behave themselves. As the train moves out there is always a scramble between the people who have got out and do not want to be left behind, and the people who are kodaking up to the last minute. Crossing the prairie, every operator imagines he is going to kodak an Indian; but the wily Indian sits in the shade, where instantaneous photography availeth not, and, if he observes himself being "time exposed," covers himself with a blanket.

A good selection of photographs was also available from numerous photographic firms, such as Boorne & May of Calgary or Trueman & Caple of Vancouver, who made much of their livelihood by selling viewbooks of scenery on the line. As well, the company continued to sell its own portfolios, *Glimpses Along The Canadian Pacific Railway, Mountain Series A* and *Indian Series A,* in its hotels and on the train.

Another service for tourists, instituted in an informal way by the CPR in 1893, provided guides for hotel patrons who desired to hunt, fish or explore the mountains away from the main line. Tom Wilson, a former packer on the CPR survey and the man credited with the discovery of both Lake Louise and Emerald Lake in 1882, had in the years after the completion of the line performed some odd jobs, such as trail-making, for the CPR. When the hotel manager received requests for guides and outfits from visiting sportsmen he put them in touch with Wilson, who had a number of horses at a homestead in the foothills east of the mountains. Over the years this business increased greatly and in the early 1890s Wilson acquired a corral site on Banff Avenue, the main street of the resort town, as a local headquarters. In 1893 he gained the company's permission to advertise himself as "Guide to the CPR." By the late 1890s even his outfitting headquarters had become a tourist attraction and one of the early tourist-explorers in the mountains, Walter Wilcox, described the attention they received:

During the summer season 'Wilson's' is frequently the scene of no little excitement when some party is getting ready to leave. Then you may see ten or fifteen wicked-eyed ponies, some in a corral and the rest tied to trees ready for packing. If the horses are making their first trip of the season there will be considerable bucking and kicking before all is ready. Several men are seen bustling about, sorting and weighing the packs, and making order out of the pile of blankets, tents, and bags of flour or bacon. The cayuses are saddled and cinched up one by one with many a protesting bite and kick. The celebrated 'diamond hitch' is used in fastening the packs, and the struggling men look picturesque in their old clothes and sombreros as they tighten the ropes, bravely on the gentle horses, but rather gingerly when it comes to a bucking bronco.

A crowd of the businessmen of Banff, who usually take about 365 holidays every year, stands around to offer advice and watch the sport. Then the picturesque train of horses with

Watching the colourful packers at work in Wilson's corral was a popular tourist pastime at Banff. Tom Wilson is at the right

their wild looking drivers files out through the village streets under a fussillade of snap-shot cameras and the wondering gazes of new arrivals from the east.

A colourful character who would gain a reputation as Canada's foremost mountain man, Wilson constituted a powerful public relations force in CPR tourism over a period of more than fifty years. He also invented a tourist attraction at Banff that would entertain generations of CPR patrons. In June, 1894, when the flooding waters of the Bow River washed out several miles of track, W.L. Mathews went to Tom for ideas on how to entertain the stranded guests at the Banff Springs Hotel. Realizing the fascination of tourists with Indians, Wilson suggested that the neighbouring Stoneys be asked to participate in a series of contests for prizes to be put up by the CPR. He travelled to the Stoney reserve at Morley as the company's emissary and

convinced the Indians of the benefits of his plan. A large contingent followed him to Banff, where the braves competed in horse races, bucking and roping competitions and traditional dancing while the women vied to outdo each other in horse packing and tepee pitching. The hotel guests were so taken with the performance that the CPR, with the assistance of local businessmen, sponsored Banff Indian Days as an annual event, expanding it to include parades and other competitions.

Although the federal government and the CPR cooperated to initiate tourist-oriented development at Banff, the task was left almost entirely to the railway company in the other park reserves. The government had little money to put into the fledgling park system and chose to spend what it did have on its showpiece — Banff. On the other hand, the CPR had a vested interest in carrying out basic developments in the new reserves around Mount Stephen House and Glacier House and, within a few years, at Lake Louise as well. The company had to build rudimentary trails and bridges in these areas to cater to the new breed of tourist who began to appear at the hotels in the late 1880s. These were the mountaineers and tourist-explorers and they soon became an important part of the CPR's mountain tourist scene, requiring new facilities for their needs.

Mountaineering as an aspect of tourism had its beginnings in the 1860s when the members of the first mountaineering club, The Alpine Club (London), began to descend on Switzerland as a suitable and convenient field for their new-found alpine pursuits. Close on their heels, in 1863, were the first of Thomas Cook's Swiss excursion parties. Official Swiss tourism records give credit for the initiation of the Swiss tourist industry to these almost simultaneous occurrences. The Alpine Club's members proved to be most assiduous in their quest for "first ascents" and within a few years most of the major Swiss peaks had been conquered. The culmination of their early efforts occurred in 1865 when Edward Whymper, the foremost product of mountaineering's mid-nineteenth-century golden age, gained the summit of the Matterhorn after seven unsuccessful attempts. Thereafter English mountaineers, much like Cook's tourists, began casting their eyes further afield, looking for areas where unclimbed peaks beckoned. Their gaze first fell on the Caucasus and the Himalaya, but it was inevitable that after the completion of the CPR and the opening up of the "Canadian Alps" it would turn to the Canadian Rockies and Selkirks.

The first mountaineers to bring their alpenstocks into the CPR's vast sea of unknown mountains did so as a direct result of the railway's excursion for the British Association for the Advancement of Science in 1884. Two members of the party, the Rev. Henry Swanzy and Richard Barrington, went to the end of the line with the group and decided to complete the journey from Kicking Horse Pass to the Pacific coast by work train, horse or foot. They experienced "very consid-

erable difficulties" but succeeded in their task and returned to England full of stories of the wondrous scenery they had seen. Swanzy's cousin, the Irish clergyman William Spotswood Green, found that the descriptions "awakened my interest and caused visionary desires to rise in my mind that some day or other, I too might have a chance of seeing those vast pine forests, with their grand background of glacier-clad peaks." After the completion of the CPR, Green noted all the travellers' accounts about the glories of the mountains and assumed they "were pretty well done" as a field for mountaineering. But, as luck would have it, he met the artist from *The Graphic* who had been on the British Association's 1884 excursion and he, in turn, had recently been in communication with the botanist John Macoun. Macoun had mentioned that the Selkirks remained virtually unexplored and awaited experienced climbers. As a member of The Alpine Club and the Royal Geographical Society, Green had climbed with an earlier expedition to the Southern Alps of New Zealand.

Green arrived in Canada with Swanzy in July, 1888, and tried to contact Van Horne, with whom he had been in correspondence, about his plans. The vice-president was unavailable, but had foreseen the potential benefits of Green's expedition and provided two free passes to Vancouver and return with stopover privileges in the mountains as well as a letter of introduction to Richard Marpole. The letter instructed Marpole to attempt to find some "active, handy reliable fellows" to assist the clergymen in their mountaineering exploits and to "give them the benefit of your experience in and knowledge of the mountains, and assist them in any way you can." Quickly departing for the west, the two arrived at Glacier House after an uneventful journey and began to prepare for a month's climbing and exploration.

At the time Green and Swanzy arrived no recorded railway tourist had penetrated the wilderness away from the CPR line. In 1887 the Vaux family of Philadelphia had decided to return home on the Canadian Pacific after visiting Yellowstone Park and had stopped for a short visit at Glacier House. The two scientifically-oriented boys in the family, George and William, had become interested in the Illecillewaet Glacier and took photographs and measurements of its tongue, but time had not allowed them to explore further. With four weeks ahead of them, Green and Swanzy, working out of Glacier House and camps established farther afield, applied themselves to their primary objective, the production of a map of the area immediately south of the CPR line by means of plane-table surveys and photographs. Their first test was the lofty Mount Sir Donald, where they failed to gain the summit but achieved a high altitude and an excellent point from which to begin their survey. Shortly after, they succeeded in climbing the neighbouring Mount Bonney, which they named, and also examined Asulkan Glacier and Pass, which they also named. During their return trip eastward, they stopped at Laggan for a short trip to Lake Louise. Finding no discernible trail, they bushwhacked as best they could and, after becoming separated from Swanzy, Green found the outlet stream and followed it to the lake. His reaction was similar to that of millions of tourists who would follow him: "I was quite unprepared for the full beauty of the scene. Nothing of the kind could possibly surpass it. I was somewhat reminded of the Oeschinen See in Switzerland, but Lake Louise is about twice as long, the forests surrounding it are far richer, and the grouping of mountains is simply perfection."

Green's trip to the Selkirks and Rockies produced two very significant developments in CPR tourism. On returning to the east, he and Swanzy stopped in Montreal to tell Van Horne of the wonders they had seen. Van Horne, impressed with what Green reported, wrote to William Whyte to tell him of the mountaineer's suggestions:

The Rev. Mr. Green, who has been investigating the Glaciers etc. in the Selkirks, reports that Lake Louise, opposite and near Laggan, is probably the most interesting spot on our line and while being not very far from Banff will afford a very desirable place for excursions from the Banff hotel. The more we have of such plans the better.

He says all through the Summer season avalanches come down into the lake at very frequent intervals — a good many of them in the afternoon — and this will be a matter of special

Green's impression of Lake Louise from *Among the Selkirk Glaciers*

interest to tourists. He reports that the ground is very favourable for a bridle path from Laggan to the Lakes and that very little work would have to be done. He thinks it might be made practicable for wheeled vehicles as the rise is very gradual.

It might be well to put up a chalet and provide some boats there, before another season...

I would be glad if you will look into this matter before winter sets in and ascertain what the expense of making the road would be, and find a good location on the lake for a chalet.

We would have to provide a few sleeping bunks, and a small kitchen as a good many visitors would probably stay overnight.

This view of the first CPR chalet at Lake Louise appeared briefly in company tourist literature

By 1890 a small log building had been erected by CPR crews on almost the spot where Green had viewed the lake. The idea behind the first Lake Louise Chalet, as Van Horne had indicated, was merely to provide shelter and overnight accommodation for those adventurous enough to make it to the lake. To enable them to do so, a rough wagon road was constructed by the CPR in 1891 making connection with the station at Laggan. The original log chalet burned down early in 1893, causing the CPR to re-assess the development at Lake Louise. The new chalet, built on the same site the following year, was a frame structure more in the mode of a hotel. This description was provided by Charles E. Fay, a visitor during its second year of operation:

In its initial stage the little structure — a single storey with a hip roof — contained in all only eight rooms including the principal one, whose plate glass windows looked out on Mt. Victoria, not as yet named, and the changeful lake. It served as office, dining room, drawing room and even bar, and on this occasion one of its corners furnished my sleeping quarters; for our party of twenty quite exceeded the Chalet's capacity, several being relegated to tents. Remaining in possession for several days, it is hardly too much to infer that for the general C.P.R. tourists of that year we were most unpopular.

Willoughby Astley, manager of the chalet, hired some Stoney Indians to act as guides and build bridle trails around the lake and up to the nearby Lake Agnes. Astley welcomed only fifty guests to the limited quarters available in the first season, but expanded facilities would soon attract increased patronage. The construction of the chalet was the CPR's first attempt to exploit the tourist potential of the mountain wilderness away from the main line and was a significant commitment to the development of holiday destinations in the mountains.

The second effect of Green's expedition was the attraction of mountaineers and explorers to the Rockies and Selkirks. When he returned to England he prepared papers for both the Royal Geographical Society and The Alpine Club, enlightening some of his fellow members on the challenge of the Canadian mountains for the first time. Even more important was the publication of his book *Among the Selkirk Glaciers* with its accompanying map in 1890, the first account by a CPR tourist to concentrate on the mountain wilderness off the main line. Its status can be measured by the report of a visitor to Glacier House in 1891 who found a group of mountain enthusiasts "accustomed to gather every evening around a blazing fire and read selections from Green's 'Among the Selkirk Glaciers' just as our forefathers were wont to read a daily chapter from the Bible."

Green's inspiration quickly provided the CPR with a great many other explorers who wrote their own accounts and attracted still more adventurers.

In 1893 a Chicago paper manufacturer, Robert L. Barrett, went on a three-week outing with CPR Land Commissioner L.A. Hamilton, and on returning hired Tom Wilson to guide him to the impressive Mount Assiniboine, soon to be advertised as "the Matterhorn of the Rockies," south of Banff. The same summer two Yale University students, Walter D. Wilcox and Samuel E.S. Allen, approached Wilson to supply them with "outfit" so that they could attempt the first ascents of Mounts Temple and Victoria at Lake Louise. In 1894 Wilcox and Allen returned to Lake Louise with three of their classmates and accomplished the first in-depth exploration of the area, including the discoveries of Paradise and Prospector's Valleys and the Valley of the Ten Peaks. Returning from the first ascent of Mount Temple they met Charles E. Fay, a professor at Tufts College in Massachusetts and president of

Wilcox, Allen and their Yale classmates spent an idyllic summer in 1894 camping, exploring and climbing in the vicinity of Lake Louise. W. D. Wilcox photograph

the Appalachian Mountain Club of Boston. The following year, 1895, Fay led an excursion of twenty Appalachian Club members, many of them women, to Lake Louise to try some of the easier climbs in the vicinity. Three of the party, Fay, Philip S. Abbot and Charles S. Thompson, then engaged Wilson for a trip to the north to accomplish the first ascent of Mount Hector. Each year the frontier was pushed further back. In 1897 Wilson outfitted Professor Jean Habel, a member of the German-Austrian Alpine Club, on the first trip up the Yoho Valley as far as the Yoho Glacier, and the next year Wilson provided the means for a party led by Professor J. Norman Collie, a member of The Alpine Club, to discover the Columbia Icefield. Because of the growing importance of alpinists, the company did everything in its power to help them in their pursuits, occasionally providing a handcar or allowing them to ride free on freight trains to the point on the line nearest their proposed ascent.

These early mountaineers were the type of tourist the Passenger Traffic Department coveted — the return visitor. Walter Wilcox undoubtedly held the record, beginning his visits to the Rockies in 1891, returning in 1893 and then, with a few exceptions, coming back every summer until his death in 1950. Charles Fay was not far behind, reporting in 1922 that he had been in the mountains every year but one since 1894. Glacier House and its environs had its own devotees, notably George and William Vaux and their sister Mary, the Philadelphia Quakers who first visited the hotel in 1887. On a second visit in 1894 they were amazed at the changes that had taken place in the glacier and were astounded by movements apparent from observations made during their third visit in 1897. Fascinated by the recession they noted, they returned annually until 1906 making observations, measurements and photographic records to explain the movement scientifically. Many of the visits were made on CPR passes and the railway supported the publication of the family's pamphlet, *The Glaciers of the Canadian Rockies and Selkirks*, which first appeared about 1900. Friends of the Vaux family, Dr. Charles Schäffer and his wife, Mary, who had met at Glacier House, began a decade of trips to Glacier in 1891 to investigate the botany of the region. Dr. Schäffer died in 1903 but his wife carried on his work with the assistance of Dr. Stewardson Brown and it was published in 1907 under the title *Alpine Flora of the Canadian Rocky Mountains*. The latter part of the nineteenth century was the era of the dedicated amateur in the natural sciences, and many other tourist-explorers with similar interests were repeat mountain visitors as well.

Climbers also began to frequent Glacier House in increasing numbers after Green's initial work, varying greatly in the amount of expertise they brought to the task. There quickly arose a call for competent guides to assist them. The point was perhaps best made by Dr. J.H. Stallard, an English physician

teaching in the Medical School at the University of California, who had toured the Alps as early as 1852. In 1894 he paid his first visit to the Rockies and Selkirks, returning in 1896. Subsequently he wrote to David McNicoll, now passenger traffic manager, and suggested that the CPR pay more attention to promoting the country away from the main line:

> *The scenery of these excursions in my opinion equals if it does not exceed any to be found in Switzerland, and it has the greater advantage of not being overrun with Hotels, Guides and Railways. It seems to me a thousand pities, however, that the attractions of these mountains are so little known. Thousands pass through them with nothing but a passing glance from the observation car, and without a suspicion of the sublimity of what they leave behind them. It was almost an accident which arrested my journey at Laggan, and kept me for more than a week at Lake Louise. Passengers on your road are compelled to see the Gorge of the Fraser River and the wonders of the Kicking Horse Pass, if forest fires permit it, but not one in a thousand ever hears of the sublimity of Mt. Temple or the glorious Panorama of Mt. Abbott to pass which without a visit is an artistic sin...*

Stallard went on to point out other deficiencies and also suggested some solutions:

> *At none of the Hotels is there much practical interest in mountain climbing. There are no visitors' books in which the travellers may record their experiences, their impressions of the scenery, their excursions, their accounts of guides, weather, etc. etc. The traveller arrives, the weather is unpropitious. Without some encouragement he leaves disgusted by the next train, but if he reads of some one who has waited for a few hours and been rewarded by a glorious view, he too remains, and instead of disgust carries away memories which will endure for life...*
>
> *A great defect of the district is the almost complete absence of well qualified guides. No large excursion can now be made without danger... I would rather trust a Swiss guide on a mountain he had never seen than any man I saw in the Rockies who had been there half his life. The best Swiss guides earn in the season from 8 to 10 francs a day and there are scores who would jump at a contract for constant employment at much less. I would therefore suggest the importation of a good Swiss guide from Chamounix or Zermatt to conduct visitors to the more difficult points of view, and in the off*

season to supervise the construction and repair of trails...

McNicoll sent a copy of Stallard's letter to T.G. Shaughnessy, then vice-president, with the following comment: "As you know I have all along been of the opinion that we must provide increased accommodation and facilities in the mountains if we expect people to visit them *and stay among them*, and I understand a little has been done at Louise, but I think a great deal more needs to be done." It took a few years for any new facilities to appear but in the meantime improvements were made to the Lake Louise Chalet, Mount Stephen House and Glacier House. In 1902 the CPR took its first step in developing the wilderness potential of the Yoho Park Reserve by building two rough log cabins with canvas roofs on the shore of Emerald Lake, the forerunners of the Emerald Lake Chalet. At Glacier the company built some crude shelters for mountaineers and explorers about 1900 on the Avalanche Crest trail and at Observation Point near Marion Lake. A more substantial log shelter was the Hermit or Rogers Hut built for the use of mountaineers at the end of the Hermit trail in 1902.

By the 1897 season the visitors' book at Glacier House had been established, and soon afterwards a register was installed at the Lake Louise Chalet. Meanwhile, a request had been sent to the CPR office in London to investigate the possibility of hiring Swiss guides. Someone in the office was acquainted with an English émigré named Clarke living in the town of Interlaken. Clarke received a letter from the CPR giving him authority to hire two guides and through his son Charles, who could speak German and was himself a qualified guide, he approached Edward Feuz, the chief guide of the district. Feuz agreed to go and persuaded his friend and fellow guide Christian Häsler to accompany him.

Their trip to Canada in the spring of 1899 was a publicity man's dream. The CPR put the guides, dressed in full climbing gear, on parade in public places in London. On their arrival in Montreal more public appearances were scheduled, including a climb staged in a local stone quarry. The great rush of free advertising reinforced the CPR's "Swiss" theme and it continued after the guides' arrival at Glacier House. In fact, they may have done more promotional work than guiding in their first year, posing for pictures with delighted tourists and through their interpreter, Charles Clarke, answering questions for visitors and newspapermen.

The climbers were pleased to have the guides, even at the rather steep price of $5.00 a day, and the guides were equally pleased to be able to show their worth. Charles Fay, the first to use the guides on a climb of Mount Dawson, found them eager to get on with their job when he arrived at Glacier House on August 3:

I believe I may assert with no immodesty that my advent was a source of unmixed pleasure to at least two of the varied company gathered on the platform to witness the event of the evening, the arrival of "No. 1" — as the west-bound overland train is commonly designated. I refer to the two unique-looking, bronze-faced men, who, religious in the performance of their duty, paced the platform during those important half-hours in hob-nailed shoes, pipe in mouth, and otherwise attired as the regulation Swiss guides. No pair of twin brothers were more nearly duplicates in raiment, no two guides ever more effectively supplemented the one the other in excellences than did Christian Häsler and Edward Feuz of Interlaken. Glad they were, for they were longing for more entertaining labors than these promenades, and the hardly

Swiss guides Edward Feuz and Christian Häsler pose in full regalia shortly after their arrival at Glacier House in 1899.
Vaux family photograph

bolder ones that constituted the chief of their function, the guiding of tourists to the foot of the Illecillewaet Glacier, with the possible roping up for short trips on the ice-foot itself.

Although the ascents the two guided the first year were fairly straightforward, the railway was well pleased with both their work and their advertising value. Consequently, the next year Feuz was asked to bring three more guides from Interlaken to work with him at Glacier House while Christian Häsler was transferred to Mount Stephen House.

Quickly realizing that it was on to something good with the Swiss guides, the CPR became receptive to other suggestions for promoting the mountains. The most interesting but most troublesome promotion featured the most prominent name in mountaineering, Edward Whymper, who first visited Canada in 1900 at the invitation of the company. After completing his transcontinental trip he approached the president with a plan for a series of climbs in the mountains, to be followed by publication of accounts of his exploits in English newspapers and journals. In return the CPR would provide free transportation, lodging and assistance for himself and his retinue of four Swiss guides. Robert Kerr, who had succeeded McNicoll as passenger traffic manager in 1899, was assigned to Whymper and arranged for a trip in 1901. It turned out to be one of the few times that a company promotional scheme backfired. Whymper, past his prime at sixty-two and rumoured to be alcoholic, was extremely difficult to handle. In the course of expeditions in 1901, 1903 and 1904 he spent more time criticizing CPR personnel, facilities and services than he did mountaineering. However, he did write for *The Times* some very positive things about the Rockies and their possibilities for mountaineering and coined a term — "fifty Switzerlands in one" — that quickly became a catch-phrase in CPR publicity.

During this period much of the promotional material produced by the company dealt specifically with the mountains, a direct result of the decision to develop them as a destination rather than promoting them as scenery en route to somewhere else. A folder entitled *Banff Springs Canadian National Park,* which made its debut in the early 1890s, was the first of the type to appear. Illustrated with both photographs and engravings in the style of earlier CPR promotional materials, it featured information under such headings as "Banff the Beautiful" and "The Lakes in the Clouds" (Lake Louise and Lake Agnes). Particular attention was paid to "The Medicinal Hot Springs," promoted in the manner of a European spa: "Though Banff is chiefly a resort of tourists and pleasure seekers, its waters have properties that are commended strongly by medical men. Dr. Danter, pres't of the American Health Resort Association, says: 'The springs are natural hot sulphur water, combining other chemical ingredients, and while the air is a restorer to the pulmonary diseased, the springs are particularly beneficial to rheumatic patients as to those afflicted in some other ways.'" Included in the information on the water was an analysis of its mineral content "made by Prof. Osler, of Philadelphia, in 1886." Other sections of the folder described things for tourists to do and see in the vicinity of Banff and Lake Louise, the "CPR Chalet Hotels" at Field, Glacier and North Bend and, of course, the delights of the Banff Springs Hotel.

Complementing the *Banff Springs* folder was another entitled *Banff and the Lakes in the Clouds in the Canadian Rockies,* which began appearing about 1893. It included virtually all the same material with the addition of maps of Rocky Mountains Park and the Yoho Park Reserve, a map of trails in the Lake Louise area, and, with the growing influence of mountaineering, later editions had sections entitled "Mountain Climbing" and "Swiss Guides." The most elaborate production was a ninety-two-page booklet, *The Challenge of the Mountains,* which made its appearance shortly after the turn of the century. Replete with over fifty tastefully produced photographs and sporting the first CPR full-colour cover, it took the more traditional approach of describing the country beginning in Calgary and moving westward to the Pacific coast. *The Challenge of the Mountains* was an expensive production and graphically illustrated how important the mountains had become in the CPR's tourism campaign.

The *Empress of India* docks at Vancouver on April 28, 1891 on the CPR's first "globe circling excursion" to be greeted by a proud Van Horne. Baily Bros. photograph

VI: The Imperial Highway

The success of Van Horne's tourist campaign was obvious by 1890. In a few years Canada had become familiar to travellers the world over and the number of tourists was steadily increasing, although there were to be some disappointments with the onset of a world depression early in the decade. It is difficult to measure the success statistically, but there are some figures available that give an idea of its acceptance. For example, passengers carried increased from 1,791,034 in 1886 to 3,009,015 in 1894, figures that should take into account the substantial number of emigrants heading for the west. The increase in the number of first-class sleeping and dining cars acquired is a more specific indicator of tourist traffic. When transcontinental service began the company had forty-seven sleeping and dining cars, by 1890 it owned sixty-one and in 1894, when the effects of the depression began to be felt severely, it possessed ninety-nine, a number that remained constant until 1898. In terms of earnings, CPR annual reports lumped gross earnings of sleeping and parlour cars together, again both of these operations being closely associated with the tourist trade. Such earnings increased from $118,659 in 1886 to $268,097 in 1890 and then to $331,720 in 1894, where they remained more or less static until 1898.

Van Horne had kept control of publicity in his own hands, corresponding with artists, photographers, tourists and excursion groups and overseeing the design and production of promotional material. However, when he become president after George Stephen's resignation in 1888, Van Horne was forced to delegate some of his workload. In 1893 he turned publicity over to David McNicoll, although his fine hand could still be seen to be working in the background. McNicoll had been one of the company's hardest workers since joining the CPR in 1883 as general passenger agent for the Eastern Division. At the time Van Horne gave him his new responsibilities he was general passenger agent for all lines, in 1896 he was passenger traffic manager, in 1899 assistant general manager

and in 1900 second vice-president and general manager. Van Horne had also recruited the man who was to assist McNicoll immeasureably, the flamboyant former newspaperman George Ham, to whom credit must go for founding the first CPR publicity department.

A measure of Ham's ingenuity, which he was to exhibit throughout his career with the CPR, can be gained from his own description of one of his early contacts with the company as a reporter on the first transcontinental train:

The first through train to cross the continent in Canada left Montreal on June 28th, 1886, and reached the western terminus, Port Moody, right on the dot on July 4th... There were only two sleepers attached and they were comfortably filled. The only newspaperman aboard was myself, and I had written up the trip from Montreal to Winnipeg in advance, and sent it by mail — for I had been on the road frequently — only adding the names of the more prominent passengers by wire from Ottawa. When the papers reached us on the north shore of Lake Superior, Mr. Dewey, the superintendent of the postal service in Canada, who was on board, was astonished at the length and accuracy of my report, and wondered how and when I had written it, and as I did not enlighten him, except to say that he had seen me writing on the train, his mystification remained with him until his death.

At the time Ham was an employee of the *Manitoba Free Press*, having moved to Winnipeg from Trenton, Ontario, where he had been born in 1847 and had learned the printing trade. On arrival in Winnipeg he had applied at the paper for a job as printer, and the foreman of the office, Frank Oliver, the future founder of the *Edmonton Bulletin* and Minister of the Interior, gave an account of his appearance: "A young fellow just up from Ontario blew in, told a joke or two, and asked for a job at the case. I liked his jokes and his style, and gave him the job and some good advice." Soon the paper's editor, W.F. Luxton, noticed that there were certain humourous articles appearing anonymously in his columns, and immediately appointed the author, Ham, to the editorial staff. In a few years Ham became the city editor and gained fame with his jocular "Locals" column, often picked up by large eastern newspapers. In 1883

he was elected to the first of three terms he would serve on Winnipeg City Council.

Ham had been a notable defender of the CPR and its policies in his column, probably bringing him to Van Horne's attention. On visiting Winnipeg the president decided to meet the company's staunch supporter and "immediately surrendered unconditionally to the charm of Ham's remarkable personality," hiring him on the spot. At the time, July, 1891, he was placed on the payroll as a general passenger agent but in 1893

Imaginative ticket-selling schemes were devised during the depression years to increase tourist usage of the CPR's eastern lines

he received the newly created position of journalist. This was essentially the beginning of what would become known as the Canadian Pacific Press Bureau.

Throughout his career with the CPR, Ham insisted that he had no official title, but those with whom he came in contact supplied him with several unofficial ones. Sir Thomas White once referred to him as "a great national asset," *Collier's Magazine* identified him as "the greatest unprinted wit in Canada," another report called him "the Mark Twain of Canada," and a writer for *The Railroad Man's Magazine* named him "Ambassador-At-Large for the Canadian Pacific Railway," perhaps the most accurate appellation, for he was called upon to be constantly on the move. A contemporary biographical sketch states that "the last place in the world to look for Ham with any reasonable hope of finding him is at his office." In addition to preparing publicity, he squired parties of journalists or other special excursions across the country, spoke at dinners and public functions, represented the company at fairs and expositions and entertained special guests. And, as *The Railroad Man's Magazine* reported, he was a master at his job:

Wherever the strangers hail from, they always go home filled with enthusiasm for Canada, for that is the end and aim of Ham's existence. If there are any statistics, scraps of general information which lend color or good stories about the Dominion that Ham doesn't know, you may be sure that they don't count. Also the visitors carry home a cordial esteem for their host.

His tact is boundless, his equanimity unassailable, his flow of quaint humor is inexhaustible as a mountain brook. His fame as a wit and an after-dinner speaker has been carried around the world by home-going travelers. He has even been made the hero of a poem by Neill Munroe, which relates "How Laughter Came To Canada."

To maintain his fund of fact and fable, Ham kept up a stable of sources across the country. For example, Tom Wilson, his source for mountain material, often telegraphed matters of regional interest to him. When the CPR was requested to supply specimens of native animals by scientific and museological institutions around the world, as it frequently was, Ham called on Wilson to provide them.

Numerous anecdotes are told about Ham and his public relations abilities during the last decade of the nineteenth and the first two of the twentieth century. One, which he later partly denied, was related in *The Railroad Man's Magazine* and concerned a party of Canadian women journalists on an excursion to the coast who visited a Mormon settlement in Alberta en route:

Soon after the party had started, some depraved person around headquarters conceived the idea that it would be a great joke to send this telegram purporting to come from L.O. Armstrong, the colonization agent, to the Mormon bishop at Lethbridge, Alberta, the centre of a large Mormon settlement:

"George Ham, rich Mormon from Wyoming, with fifteen wives in private car, will arrive Lethbridge, Thursday, 12th, for a new location; advise that he be treated well in hope he may decide to settle. He would be most valuable acquisition to the colony.

L.O. Armstrong
Colonization Agent, CPR"

When the train with the journalists' car arrived at Lethbridge, the entire Mormon population, attired in Sunday clothes and headed by the bishop and elders, were drawn up on the station platform to receive the visiting brother and his fifteen wives. Ham was much perplexed by the unexpected warmth of his greeting.

Not until some of the brethren began to question him about his various marriages, desiring particularly to know just where and how he had managed to corral such an all-star connubial galaxy, did it dawn on him that somebody had been trying to play a joke. But he was game. He carried out the role that had been thrust upon him and departed among the affectionate adieus of the brethren, promising to return and buy some land after keeping an important engagement in Moose Jaw.

The efforts of Ham and all of those who worked with McNicoll in the Passenger Traffic Department were sorely needed during the depression of the nineties to maintain the tourist business. Facing a decline in overseas traffic, the department renewed its "Summer Tour" promotion to increase Canadian and American tourism. Creative ideas were introduced in ticketing to compete with American lines that were vying for the same customers. On portions of the line east of Sault Ste. Marie they could buy a thousand-mile ticket, good for a year, for $25.00, a round-trip first-class ticket good for a month at a one-sixth reduction, a season ticket at reduced rates good for one round

Nepigon Bay from Nepigon Station

trip a day between any two stations for periods varying from one to twelve months, or Saturday excursion tickets good for return the following Monday from cities to points within a sixty-mile radius at ten cents more than a one-way first-class rate. For sportsmen travelling anywhere on the line in parties of five or more, a one-month return-trip ticket was available at reduced rates. Included in this offer was the free transfer of 200 pounds of baggage and camp equipment, consisting of tents, canoes under twenty feet in length, and camp utensils, as well as fifty pounds of fish and game. Special round-trip excursion fares were also available to parties of eight or more travelling together.

Another popular means of attracting Canadian and American tourists during these years was the personally-conducted tour, a throwback to the system first operated by Thomas Cook. Typical of these was the Alaska tour offered in 1897. Beginning from Boston and New York, the thirty-five-day tour cost an expensive $375, giving it a very exclusive appeal, but it offered the best in transportation, accommodation, convenience and service that was available: "The Canadian Pacific Ry. Tour to Alaska will be 'personally conducted' by an experienced representative of the Passenger Traffic Department, who will look after the comfort of passengers in every possible way, and the advantages of travelling with a party of this description are readily apparent when it is remembered that one is relieved of all trouble about securing his hotel accommodations or steamship berths, looking after baggage or planning what he shall do next." The tour included stopovers at key points — Montreal, Banff and Glacier — before passage was taken on the thirteenth day on the Pacific Coast Steamship Company's *Queen*. The steamer paid brief calls at Wrangell and Juneau before visiting Glacier Bay for views of the magnificent Muir Glacier, "a wall of ice nearly two miles long and several

Personally conducted tours to Alaska were a popular attraction helping to achieve utilization of the CPR's transcontinental lines during the nineties

hundred feet high, and rising in a glittering cliff out of the waves…formed by the union of twenty-six tributary glaciers, and the united mass of ice covers an area of 1,000 square miles." On the twenty-third day the *Queen* arrived back at Tacoma, from where the passengers proceeded by ship to Seattle to board the Great Northern Railway for the trip back east with stopovers at Lake Minnetonka, Minnesota, and, through connecting lines, Niagara Falls, New York. Tours of this kind were very fashionable at the time and the company had little trouble filling their complement.

In the same period the CPR launched a campaign aimed at promoting Canadian tourism as part of a round-the-world tour scheme. The downturn in the economy occurred at a time when the CPR's initial overseas tourist promotion program seemed to be losing steam. The English market had been more or less saturated, as Van Horne noted in a letter written in 1892 to the Rev. J.J. Lewis of Boston, who had requested sponsorship for his English lecture tour: "While your new lecture would undoubtedly do much good in England if delivered just in the right time and place and under circumstances to make it attract the attention of those who travel, there is now hardly a man, woman or child in England who is not pretty well acquainted with the Canadian Pacific, and some of our people over there are strongly of the opinion that a good many of our recent expenditures towards making it better known have been unnecessary." After stimulating the

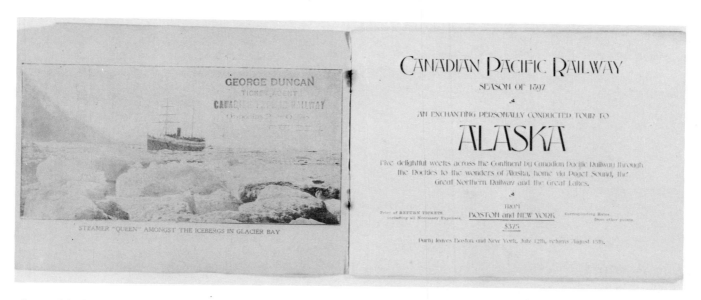

STEAMER "QUEEN" AMONGST THE ICEBERGS IN GLACIER BAY

GEORGE DUNCAN
TICKET AGENT
CANADIAN PACIFIC RAILWAY

CANADIAN PACIFIC RAILWAY

SEASON OF 1897

AN ENCHANTING PERSONALLY CONDUCTED TOUR TO

ALASKA

Five delightful weeks across the Continent by Canadian Pacific Railway through the Rockies to the wonders of Alaska, home via Puget Sound, the Great Northern Railway and the Great Lakes.

Price of RETURN TICKETS
including all Necessary Expenses

FROM
BOSTON and NEW YORK
$375

Corresponding Rates
from other points

Party leaves Boston and New York, July 12th, returns August 15th.

British market with its "mountain campaign," the company made a new pitch promoting the all-British route, or Imperial Highway, to the Orient and around the world.

Van Horne had once stated that Canada was in a backwater and that it was his objective to put it on a highway, a dream shared by George Stephen, who envisaged the CPR as part of a larger Imperial transportation system. In 1889 the company took a major step in this direction by placing an order for three 6,000-ton vessels with the Naval Construction and Armaments Company of Barrow. The three, the *Empress of India, Empress of Japan* and *Empress of China*, built to replace the smaller chartered steamers the company was using on the Pacific, enabled the CPR to reach an agreement on an Imperial mail contract in 1890. The contract called for a mail subsidy of £60,000 annually in return for a transit time not to exceed 684 hours from Hong Kong to Quebec in summer and 732 hours from Hong Kong to Halifax in winter. But the three Empresses were also designed to provide the best passenger service available on the Pacific. The promotional material for them, not surprisingly, echoed the familiar themes of the company's transcontinental rail service:

THEY ARE THE ONLY TWIN-SCREW STEAMSHIPS ON ANY PACIFIC LINE and they have all the modern improvements and latest appliances known to marine architecture to insure speed, safety and comfort. The hulls are of steel, with double bottoms extending the full length of the vessel, and are divided into numerous watertight compartments, rendering them practically unsinkable. The engines (10,000 horsepower) have developed a speed of over nineteen knots. The saloons, library and staterooms are marvels of beauty and luxury. They are lighted throughout by electricity, are thoroughly well ventilated and for comfort excel anything afloat.

The advertising campaign for the CPR's round-the-world tours was launched long before the first ship, the *Empress of India,* was completed in January, 1891. In addition to a major newspaper campaign, the company issued a brochure, *Around the World, Globe Circling Excursions Arranged by the Canadian Pacific Railway,* which proclaimed: "As the vessels are superbly appointed for passengers…and must take their station on the Pacific, the Railway Company decided to offer the travelling public a trip round the world, the entire journey to be made in Canadian Pacific Steamships and Trains, excepting only the voyage across the Atlantic, which may be made via Montreal, Quebec, New York or Boston, in the steamships of the Transatlantic Lines." There was space for 170 Saloon passengers on each of the ships and the basic fare was set at £120 ($600), including meals and berths while travelling at sea or on the CPR line but not including expenses ashore, on rail lines other than the CPR or during stopovers at the "Canadian Pacific Mountain Hotels." Passengers were invited to join the tour at its starting point in Liverpool, at Naples or at any point in Canada and the United States served by the CPR or its connecting lines, and reduced fares were offered to those wishing to start the tour at Liverpool and leave it in North America.

sident was at the dock to meet her. Other transportation men hailed the tour as a great achievement because it was the first steamship tour of the world under the direction of one company. Chauncey Depew, president of the Vanderbilt-controlled New York Central & Hudson River Railroad, put the accomplishment in an interesting perspective: "Don't talk of profits even if they do run into the thousands. The trip itself is worth half a million dollars in advertising to the Canadian Pacific."

The maiden voyages of the other Empresses were equally successful and the company quickly decided to make the round-the-world tour a permanent feature of its tourism program. Since the normal run of the three Empresses was from Vancouver to Japan and China as "the Canadian Pacific Railway's Royal Mail Steamship Line," an agreement had to be worked out with another large carrier, the Peninsular and Oriental Steam Navigation Company, the celebrated P&O, to provide the link between Britain and Hong Kong. P&O's service to India and the Orient via the Suez Canal had added to the English language the word *posh* (port outward, starboard home), an allusion to the best location of cabins through the Mediterranean and the Red Sea. Once the agreement with P&O was in place the company issued a new brochure, *Around The World By The Canadian Pacific Route*, which gave details of the schedules of the various carriers — Canadian Pacific's ships, the railway, various trans-Atlantic lines and P&O. Tours began approximately every three weeks and tourists were

Sailing from Liverpool on February 7, 1891, the *Empress of India* had a full complement of passengers, and was followed by the *Empress of Japan* on April 11 and the *Empress of China* on June 15. Ports of call included Naples, Port Said, Colombo, Penang, Singapore, Hong Kong (where a stop of ten days was planned to allow a visit to Canton), Shanghai, Kobe, Yokohama and Vancouver. At Vancouver the passenger was advised to consult the CPR brochure *The New Highway to the Orient* (a revised edition of *The New Highway to the East*) for details of his rail trip across Canada and was given the option of arriving at Montreal, Quebec, Halifax, Boston or New York to pick up overseas connections with one of several carriers.

When the *Empress of India* steamed into Vancouver flying the company's new six-square, red-and-white checkerboard house flag, which Van Horne had personally designed, the proud pre-

The Grand Saloon in the *Empress of Japan*

The steamers *Kootenay* and *Minto* unload passengers onto a waiting CPR train at Arrow Lake in 1900. Boorne and May photograph

American interests intent on bringing lines in from Washington. Similarly, in the Okanagan Valley a branch from the CPR main line at Sicamous was completed in 1893 to the north end of Okanagan Lake, where it connected with the Canadian Pacific sternwheeler *Aberdeen*, which plied the waters of the lake to Penticton, seventy miles to the south. The two lines took tourists from the transcontinental route to some of the finest summering spots in the west. In the West Kootenay the development of Halcyon Hot Springs on Arrow Lake proved attractive while in the Okanagan the salubrious climate of Penticton, Peachland and Summerland was sought by sun worshippers. At both Revelstoke and Sicamous the company built small hotels for those wishing to hunt or fish in the area or

invited to start their journey in either direction at any intermediate point on the route. The company also entered into an agreement in 1893 with Huddart, Parker and Company, an Australian firm, to use its ships *Miowera* and *Werrimeo* to operate the Canadian-Australian Steamship Line, which offered once-a-month service between Vancouver and Sydney.

As the popularity of world tours increased throughout the nineties, other advertising material was generated to help promote them. By 1893 the CPR had issued a brochure called *Westward To The Far East*, a guide to a trip across the Pacific aboard one of the company's liners that described in some detail the principal cities of Japan and China. Further expenditure on this promotion followed an analysis of the company's books that showed the Empress service was one of the few money-making aspects of the CPR's operations during the worst years of the depression between 1893 and 1896. It was also recognized that the Empresses were largely responsible for attracting tourists to Canada to use the CPR's rail services and hotels during these difficult times.

Despite the economic outlook, which was far from propitious, the company continued to develop its facilities and add rail lines, mainly to tap natural resources or to forestall competitors from the United States from building branches into Canada. Some of these lines also proved to be of interest to the tourist. For example, in 1892 the CPR built a branch line running south from Revelstoke to Arrowhead, linking with steamer service on the Columbia-Kootenay river system in southern British Columbia, in an effort to steal a march on

The Hotel Sicamous, gateway to the Okanagan Valley

those wishing to transfer to branch-line trains to the south. The Hotel Revelstoke was built immediately behind the station on a high bench of land providing a view toward Mount Begbie while the Hotel Sicamous was placed on the shore of beautiful Shuswap Lake.

The Revelstoke and Sicamous hotels were extensions, albeit minor ones, of the CPR's mountain hotel system, a successful venture despite occasional problems. Therefore it was not surprising that the company considered building hotels in other parts of the country likely to be of interest to the tourist.

The "Thunder Bay Route" on CPR steamers was continuing to be extremely popular, and in the early 1890s the Kaministiquia, essentially a scaled-down version of the Hotel Vancouver, was built at Fort William. About 1900 a small hostelry was opened at Moose Jaw, where the Soo Line connected with the CPR main line. And in 1901 the Maritimes received its first CPR hotel when the company opened a combined station and hotel at McAdam Junction, a strategic railway connecting point in New Brunswick and favourite haunt of sportsmen. But

Quebec City, transfer point in trans-Atlantic tourist travel, was destined to become the site of the CPR's most impressive hotel project to date.

Proposals for a large hotel at Quebec surfaced as early as 1880 and in 1890 a group of businessmen organized the Fortress Hotel Company and revived the idea. Probably because of the worsening economic situation they were unable to finance their plan, and in January, 1892, the Quebec City Council offered a ten-year tax exemption to any group that would take up the

Later additions to the Chateau Frontenac included the Mont Carmel wing designed by Walter Painter and built in 1908-09

project. This aroused the interest of Van Horne and others connected with the railway company, who formed the Chateau Frontenac Company and secured the lease on a piece of property adjoining the historic Dufferin Terrace. Headed by Van Horne, the group eventually had nine members, five of whom were connected with the CPR, and they quickly promised that the hotel was "to be ready for European travel *en route* to the World's Fair in Chicago" in 1893, an event the CPR was strongly promoting. Bruce Price was chosen as architect and construction, which began in May, 1892, was completed in December, 1893.

Price's creation, a horseshoe-shaped design with four wings of unequal length, was true to the chateau style he had used at Banff, with a large circular tower, turrets and dormers and an exterior of reddish-orange brick brought from Scotland. The interior was designed in the grand manner, with impressive public rooms and dining areas on the first two floors. The bedrooms were furnished with sixteenth-century-style oak furniture. Van Horne had definite ideas for the design of the hotel; before it was rendered he wrote to Stephen to advise that he would "depend on broad effects rather than ornamentation and detail. I am planning to retain the old fortifications, and keep the old guns in place, setting the hotel well back from the face of the hill so to afford ample room for a promenade, and I

think it will be the most talked-about hotel on the continent." On one occasion during construction he went out in a boat onto the St. Lawrence with Price to convince himself that the elevation as seen from the river was sufficiently majestic. His influence could be seen in the design and decor of the three impressive tower suites. One was furnished in early Quebec habitant style as a tribute to the French-Canadian population of Quebec, a second in Chinese style to represent the railway's new service to the Orient, and a third in Dutch style to recall the faith of Dutch shareholders in the line's early development and, perhaps, his own ancestry.

The developers saw the hotel primarily as a gateway to the new route to the Orient; its name evoked the memory of the seventeenth-century governor of Quebec, Count Frontenac, who had supported the westward expansion of the fur trade and La Salle's search for the overland route to Cathay. It would divert round-the-world travel to the St. Lawrence route from New York or Boston. Therefore it was not surprising that control of the venture quickly passed into the railway's hands, the CPR acquiring most of the stock in 1894 and the remainder in 1898. Like its sister hotels in the west, the Chateau Frontenac was built to generate traffic on the line, but it soon became a profitable tourist attraction on its own. An extensive advertising campaign was launched that focused attention on Quebec as an interesting tourist city. Revised editions of *The New Highway to the Orient* and *Fishing and Shooting* included etchings of the hotel and described attractions and activities in its vicinity. Also, two new brochures were issued for the 1894 season, one entitled *Quebec Summer and Winter* and the other *Historic Quebec*. The campaign was successful and as early as August, 1894, Van Horne could report to Stephen:

> The Chateau Frontenac is doing very well indeed, it has already more than made up its losses on its first six or seven months of operation — losses that all new hotels have to bear. And as near as we can figure it, it has increased our railway earnings during the summer months over $750.00 a day. It has been found quite inadequate to take care of all the summer business that has come to it, and large numbers have had to be turned away.

It was not long before the company began to think of an addition. In 1897 Price designed the Citadel Wing and Pavilion to increase the room capacity, and they were completed in 1899.

One of the CPR's new observation cars with cupolas at either end is pictured standing at Glacier House in 1903, the year after it was introduced.
Beatrise Longstaff Lance photograph

dogged it throughout much of the nineties. New equipment was being purchased and the outlook for the tourist trade was bright. For the growing number of tourists now travelling on more limited budgets, the company had introduced tourist-class sleeping cars, a less luxurious version of the first-class sleeping car, available to those with first- or second-class tickets at less than half the price of a first-class sleeper. At the turn of the century it ordered the first of a new type of observation car to supplement its three mountain observation cars, essentially ordinary day coaches with the area between the belt rail and roof left open, first introduced in 1890. The new observation car, which went into service in 1902, resembled a large caboose with a cupola at each end and a glassed-in centre section. Four of these would eventually be built and would remain in service until supplanted by new compartment sleeping cars with brass-railed observation platforms that the CPR began building in 1909. The CPR also introduced a remarkable piece of tourist equipment, called the Motor Car, to carry sightseers between Banff and Laggan stations:

The car resembles an open street car, and will comfortably seat 14 persons, although possibly 20 could be accommodated without crowding. The seats are upholstered in leather, there is a movable roof, and in the two ends are large plate glass windows, thus affording unobstructed views of the magnificent scenery of the Bow Valley. The motive power is supplied by an electro-gasoline engine, and a speed of 25 miles an hour can be attained.

By 1899 the company had added a second transcontinental train to accommodate increased passenger traffic in the summer months. Called the Imperial Limited, a name derived from the all-British route, it brought the Orient a day and a half closer, reducing transcontinental travel to 100-1/2 hours from 136.

Important as these developments were, the most significant event for the railway at the turn of the century was Van Horne's decision in 1899 to retire as president to take on the new position of chairman of the board of directors. In the thirteen years since the beginning of transcontinental service he had, with his flamboyant personality and flair for public relations, moulded a successful publicity and tourism campaign for both the company and the country. In fact it may be said that the prevailing tourist image of Canada was the one that Van Horne had chosen for the CPR.

Meanwhile, CPR officials, encouraged by the success of the Chateau Frontenac, decided to add a hotel to their proposed new station in the east end of Montreal. The Place Viger Hotel was designed by Price in 1895 and construction began in the spring of 1896. The design was reminiscent of the Chateau Frontenac's, with towers, turrets and dormers, but the facade was lighter in appearance. The ground level served as the station, the first floor as dining room and ballroom, and the remaining four floors housed the eighty-eight bedrooms. When the Place Viger Hotel opened in August, 1898, it immediately became one of the social centres of Montreal, not merely a stopover hotel for passengers using the CPR's eastern lines.

By the time the Place Viger Hotel opened its doors, the CPR was in the midst of recovering from the depression that had

A dramatic mountaineering scene with Mount Assiniboine, "the Matterhorn of the Rockies," forming the backdrop provided the illustration for this brochure

VII: The Canadian Pacific Rockies

Chosen to succeed Van Horne as president in 1899 was Thomas G. Shaughnessy, a shrewd and successful manager but an introspective man who tended to shy away from publicity. He left public relations to George Ham, and brought him into the president's office in 1903 (for what was described as "special work") to guarantee close support in the vital field of tourist promotion. Then in 1911 the president decided to reorganize the Traffic Department to create a separate branch for publicity headquartered in Montreal and Ham became its manager. Several people worked with him in this office, but there were also publicity people attached to other departments, such as the European Traffic Department in England. One of them, John Murray Gibbon, became more important than Ham himself as an image-maker for Canada and the CPR.

Gibbon was born at Udeweller, Ceylon, on April 12, 1875, the son of a Scottish teaplanter, William Duff Gibbon, who was later knighted for his service on the Legislative Council there. As was common at the time, the children were sent back to their father's home town to receive their education and young Murray attended Gordon's College and later King's College, Aberdeen, where he placed first in the English class and served as one of the editors on the school magazine. On graduation from King's College he wrote an examination for a scholarship at Christ Church, Oxford, choosing as his essay subject a topic that would interest him for the rest of his life, the relationship between poetry and music. He received the scholarship and attended Oxford for the next four years, spending several of his summers in Germany at the University of Göttingen studying, among other subjects, Sanskrit and Greek archaeology. Graduating from Oxford *summa cum laude*, he seemed destined for a life of scholarship but went to work as an apprentice for the journal *Black and White*, an offshoot of *The Graphic*. Coverage of the Boer War called for a cheaper version of the journal and Gibbon was placed in charge of the *Black and White Budget*, holding the position until tuberculosis forced him to leave for an extended rest cure in Africa. On his return to England he made a name for himself as a freelance writer with another popular journal, *The Illustrated London News*, and when a new

traffic manager, Allan Cameron, was appointed to the CPR's London office in 1907, Gibbon was recommended to him for "propaganda" services as a man who knew Fleet Street and the Continent equally well.

One of Gibbon's first assignments for the CPR came directly from Shaughnessy and it was a challenging one. He was instructed to line up twelve leading British newspaper editors to tour Canada as guests of the president. The challenge was presented by *The Times*, which prided itself on independence to the extent that it was not likely to accept such an invitation from a commercial enterprise. However, using his friendship with the English novelist Mrs. Humphrey Ward he was able to convince her husband, the chief editorial writer for *The Times*, that the invitation came not from a company but from Sir Thomas Shaughnessy, a private individual, recently knighted. As Gibbon put it, "the fish rose to the fly," and *The Times* promised to send its chief foreign editor, Ernest Brain. The other leading newspapers fell into line, not wanting to be outdone by *The Times*.

Gibbon shepherded the editors to Quebec, where he turned them over to George Ham. An account in *The Railroad Man's Magazine* describes how Ham handled the job:

Ham was assigned to escort the party over the Canadian Pacific. So anxious was the management to make a good impression that Ham was called into secret conclave and especially and particularly cautioned to be on his dignity and not to attempt any unseemly levity with such a notable assemblage.

When the party arrived in Montreal it was received by a party of distinguished citizens in the most approved English style with such frigid solemnity that ordinary travelers passing near involuntarily buttoned their coats and turned their collars up around their ears. The visitors looked as gloomy as true Britons might be expected to look on such a hospitable occasion and conversed in monosyllable.

Ham, who had purposely arrived late, greeted each visitor with his accustomed easy cordiality, and when he had been presented to all, horrified the anxious C.P.R. officials by slapping the most sedate of the great editors on the back and

John Murray Gibbon, image-maker for Canada and the CPR

calling out in a hearty invitation to "Come on boys! This way to the dining car."

With the refreshments Ham served out a continuous flow of jokes diluted to suit the British taste. Within an hour the gloom had rolled away like a fog bank before a July sun. Everybody was calling him "George" and he was addressing them by any term that came handy.

Thence forward for the eight weeks they were under Ham's charge, those Englishmen had the time of their lives. When they returned to Montreal they gave a dinner in his honor, presented him with an elaborate dressing-case, and addressed a glowing eulogy of their vicarious host to the Canadian Pacific management in a round robin.

The account did not mention that by the time the party reached Winnipeg some of the editors, Brain included, came to Gibbon and complained that they "had not expected to travel with a mere drinking party but had come to obtain information about Canada" and threatened to return home if matters were not

rectified. Gibbon approached William Whyte, vice-president of Western Lines, about the problem and Whyte agreed to attach his business car to the train and accompany it west. During the remainder of the trip Whyte spent his time with the editors, plugging the information gap and soothing their ruffled feathers.

Gibbon continued to prove his worth to the company in the course of his European publicity work. In London, his first responsibility was preparation of advertising and literature, some of it in foreign languages, to promote the company's services, but he spent as much time as possible in the field, visiting the railway's agents and offices in Great Britain and Europe. On his travels his love of music, art and literature brought him into contact with numerous important personages and his interest in culture proved to be a positive influence on their view of the CPR. His first trip to Canada had opened his eyes to the beauty of the country and the ways of its people and he persuaded the railway to let him go out each summer on an educational trip. He quickly became an authority on Canadian history and the traditions and customs of its various ethnic groups. On his Canadian trips he engaged in his pastime of marrying music and poetry, writing songs such as "Along the Wide St. Lawrence," "Quebec," "A Song of Manitoba," "The Mountie," and "Lake Louise" based on the music of old French, British, Welsh or German folk tunes.

Gibbon also shared in the job of preparing CPR exhibits, ranging in size from window displays to large-scale exhibition pavilions. He drew on his considerable knowledge of Canada to prepare a display (his first pavilion exhibit) at the Scottish National Exhibition in Glasgow in 1910, showing the role played by the Scot in the development of Canada. This pavilion received such a positive response that a London publisher approached him about writing a book on the subject, and it appeared in 1911 under the title of *Scots in Canada*, one of more than thirty works he would eventually write. Gibbon also made an important contribution to the Canadian Pacific Pavilion at White City near Shepherd's Bush in London. The building was capped by four moose guarding the globe and he provided the inscription, "Canadian Pacific Spans The World," illustrating the idea with large maps on the pavilion's exterior. It became one of the best-known slogans in Canadian railway history.

The claim was based on the CPR's successful development

Gibbon's slogan was the first to promote the CPR's world-wide passenger services

of its own fast Atlantic steamship service. An Atlantic connection had always been in the minds of Stephen and Van Horne but it remained for Shaughnessy to accomplish it. He made his first move in the steamship business in 1901 when the CPR bought the Canadian Pacific Steamship Navigation Company and ordered its first *Princess* ships to establish its own British Columbia coastal service. Noting the poor service provided by existing lines between Europe and Canada, he then decided to establish a CPR Atlantic line. As Van Horne had done previously with the Pacific service, Shaughnessy attempted to get a government mail subsidy that would underwrite some of the costs of a twenty-knot service. The government failed to support the idea, but the subsidy request publicized the CPR's desire for its own Atlantic line. Shaughnessy went ahead without the subsidy as he had CPR profits in hand for investment. In February, 1903, the company purchased from the Elder Dempster company its fleet of fifteen ships — eleven freighters with a gross tonnage of up to 10,000 and four liners whose tonnage varied from 7,400 to 9,600. Named *Lake Champlain, Lake Erie, Lake Michigan* and *Lake Manitoba*, the liners could carry between 680 and 750 passengers, about 100 of them in first-class, and saloon passage from Liverpool to Montreal started at £10. Although these vessels could achieve speeds of only twelve or thirteen knots, they provided a basic service. Advertising for round-the-world

excursions could now direct tourists to Canadian ports and CPR ships for the Atlantic part of their journey. Stephen's dream of CPR service from Liverpool to Hong Kong had become a reality, and Gibbon's slogan was soon followed by another, "Canadian Pacific, World's Greatest Travel System."

Shaughnessy moved fast to upgrade the service, placing an order with the Fairfield yards on the Clyde in November, 1904, for two luxurious liners capable of eighteen knots, the *Empress of Britain* and the *Empress of Ireland*. The two vessels went into service in 1906. Most of the passengers were third-class emigrants joining the flood heading for the Canadian west, but there were many first- and second-class passengers as well. Shaughnessy's Atlantic campaign was crowned in 1909 with the purchase of the venerable Allan Line and its eighteen steamers. The agreement was not publicly announced until 1915 and the two lines continued to operate independently in the interim. An indication of the number of potential passengers the lines brought to the CPR's railway operations is shown by figures for 1908, the year before the acquisition of the Allan Line. Westbound passengers on the eighteen Allan ships that year totalled 49,000, while the eleven ships the CPR was by then operating on the Atlantic carried 46,000.

This photograph, entitled "Leisure hours at sea, upper promenade deck," captured the typical first-class passenger on a trans-Atlantic voyage

The increasing number of tourists generated by the Atlantic line required an increase in tourist facilities in Canada. This resulted in a major expansion in the size and number of hotels, and led to the reorganization of hotel administration. For a number of years the hotels had been under the management of the superintendent of sleeping, parlor and dining cars, a post held by James Sheffield until his retirement in 1902. George

McLaren Brown, formerly executive agent, Western Lines, took over the position and held it until 1905, when he became general passenger agent, Atlantic Steamship Lines. At this point Shaughnessy established the Hotel Department and chose Hayter Reed as its manager-in-chief. Reed brought an interesting background to the position; he had served under General Sir Garnet Wolseley in the first Riel Rebellion, had been an Indian Agent at Battleford, Assistant Indian Commissioner for Manitoba and the North West Territories, a member of the North West Territories Council, and Deputy Superintendent of Indian Affairs at Ottawa. On retiring from government service he had become secretary of the St. James's Club in Montreal and then had been recruited by the CPR to manage the Chateau Frontenac. Well into his fifties by the time he became manager-in-chief of hotels, he still had the youthful energy and organizational skills required to make the system workable.

He also had an active and talented wife, Kate, who was to make as much a mark on the CPR hotels as he himself. The daughter of the Chief Justice of Ontario, John Douglas Armour, she had originally married Grosvenor Lowrey, a famous New York patent attorney who represented Thomas Edison. During the 1880s she had moved in the highest echelons of New York society, becoming both an authority on antiques and a connoisseur of paintings, and when she returned to Canada as a widow she had become advisor to many notable Canadians on their art collections, not the least of whom was William Cornelius Van Horne. Given her background, it was not surprising that after her marriage to Reed in 1894 she should put her talents to work tastefully redecorating the Chateau Frontenac. Her success in this endeavour led to a government commission to decorate the royal train that carried the Duke and Duchess of Cornwall and York across Canada in 1901, a tour that provided excellent publicity for the CPR.

In appointing Hayter Reed as manager-in-chief, Shaughnessy had in fact hired an excellent husband-and-wife team. While Reed went about the business of making the system work, his wife could take on the job of re-doing

The Duke and Duchess of Cornwall and York about to board the royal train after disembarking from the *Empress of India* at Vancouver. Kate Reed's decoration of this train in 1901 enhanced her reputation and provided the CPR with some excellent publicity

the hotels. She was allowed to travel to England and the Continent in her quest for antiques, tapestries and paintings that would meet her critical standards and expense seemed to be no object. Her first task was the Place Viger Hotel, which she transformed with the good taste she had applied to the Chateau Frontenac. She then continued to work her magic on the new hotels as they appeared during the course of the CPR's expansion program.

In 1903 two leading citizens of Victoria, Captain J.W. Troup and Harry G. Barnard, recognizing the tourist potential of their city, approached the CPR about building a hotel. After the promoters persuaded city council to grant the company an excellent site adjoining the Inner Harbour, with accompanying tax exemptions, architectural drawings were commissioned in 1904. Francis Mawson Rattenbury, who in the mid-nineties had designed the impressive nearby legislative building, created what has been called "the first separate example of the mature chateau style" in Canadian railway hotels. The Empress Hotel, completed in 1908, featured flat, unornamented walls, steep, broken roofs and Gothic dormers, recalling the lines of the Chateau Frontenac, already regarded in many circles as a great national symbol. Apparently the attempt was successful; a Victoria newspaper, *The Colonist*, called it a hotel that would "make the Western gateway of the great transcontinental system a fitting companion to the historic pile on the heights of Quebec."

The Empress Hotel commanded a strategic location on Victoria's Inner Harbour after its completion in 1908

While bringing the chateau style to its maturity at Victoria, the company was completely ignoring it in its other major hotel project at the time. The Royal Alexandra in Winnipeg, designed by Edward and William Maxwell in 1904, was a straightforward rectangular block with a flat roof. Perhaps the company made a distinction between a hotel to be promoted for tourist purposes and one to attract a commercial clientele. If so, no such distinction was applied to interior decor, for Kate Reed was directed to give both the Empress and the Royal Alexandra her utmost attention. A Winnipeg newspaper described her efforts at the Royal Alexandra in 1906:

Mrs. Hayter Reed, who has charge of the furnishings department of the C.P.R. hotel, is an elusive person to find, for she may be in any part of the great building directing and supervising the work of wall decoration, and her own especial "lair" can only be found, she avers, by a rope ladder.

When asked as to her color schemes for the hotel she laughingly said: "Oh, everything is 'blue' at present; I've such heaps to do, and so little is ready…"

Mrs. Reed naturally did not wish to have things judged when only half done, or, indeed, only begun, but a glance about made evident the fact that her marked artistic ability would be shown in the delicate harmony of the various rooms when decorated and finished.

Harmony, that is something which few of the C.P.R. hotels can boast of, for the purchasing agent has often been ordered to "get a carpet for room 196," and the carpet was got

accordingly with occasional disastrous results. Mrs. Reed does not believe that carpet and bed and bureau "furnish" a room. She will in all probability impart a touch of homeness and distinctiveness to each, and there will be nothing "haphazard" in them.

Another of her ideas is that of delicate suggestion by way of emblems. She wishes everything to be typical of the west as far as possible and this idea is carried out in the table linen, which is of the finest material, embroidered in one corner with sheaves of wheat…

The work of decorating the new hotel in Winnipeg will be along simple but most artistic lines, and could be in no better hands than those of Mrs. Reed, whose eye for color and effect is unerring and whose taste is always of the best.

The importance of Kate Reed's work to the CPR and tourism should not be underestimated since her decor was essential in establishing or maintaining the hotels as places of social distinction, particularly in the eyes of the *nouveau riche* in Canada and the United States. The hotels helped to fill the cultural vacuum in a country as new as Canada, especially in the west, and gave the customers the opportunity "to pose in the elegant costume of an age of social class, which suggested that those who entered the ballrooms of the place were invited guests of rank, gentlemen and ladies of importance, squires rather than peasants." Kate Reed's treatment of the new hotels was followed by a sweep through existing ones — the Banff Springs Hotel, the Lake Louise Chalet, Mount Stephen House, Hotel Vancouver and Glacier House. Her talent broke through the confines of interior decoration and blossomed in the landscape beyond. She designed the beautiful gardens around the Empress Hotel and introduced Iceland poppies to the grounds at Lake Louise, where they became almost as famous as the lake itself.

By the turn of the century the company had refocused its tourist promotion on its hotels. As in the case of the Chateau Frontenac, area-specific tourist advertising appeared only after a CPR hotel had been opened in the region. It happened in the Maritimes, where the company had only one hotel before 1905, a relatively minor one at McAdam Junction, N.B. In that year the Algonquin Hotel on New Brunswick's Fundy coast at St. Andrews, the locale of Van Horne's summer house, was purchased from private developers and the first major CPR tourist promotion of the region began:

> *St. Andrews is situated on Passamaquoddy Bay, and as a summer resort is not surpassed by any point on the Atlantic coast. Here the visitor finds agreeable boating and bathing facilities, numerous tennis courts and croquet lawns, an electric lighted bowling green, a splendid golf course, charming drives, enjoyable social pleasures and a salubrious climate. The Algonquin, the first of the great chain of hotels operated by the Canadian Pacific Railway across the continent, is the centre of the social life of the resort.*

Perhaps the best way to gain a measure of the interdependence of the hotel system and tourism at the beginning of the new century is by examining expansion and guest statistics at the mountain hotels. First to receive attention was the Lake Louise Chalet where, even during the depression of the nineties, the demands of mountaineers and mountain lovers were outstripping the very limited supply of guest rooms. As a result, as soon as the depression loosened its grip, F.M. Rattenbury was commissioned to plan an addition. His design kept some of the elements of the original mountain hotels but also showed the influence of the chateau style and some elements of Tudor style. Work on the long, narrow addition began about 1899, with small portions being added annually until the job was completed about 1908. At the other mountain hotels major work was not undertaken until the depression receded well into the background and the company had accumulated some much-needed capital. Although records are vague, Mount Stephen House seems to have been given a major addition in 1901-02. At Glacier House the company had built an annex in 1889 to add thirty rooms to the few in the original building, and in 1904 it commenced work on a second wing. This was completed in 1906, adding fifty-four rooms and featuring such conveniences as baths, steam heating and an elevator. The additions at both Mount Stephen House and Glacier House were in keeping with the original chalet style.

As the largest and most important of the mountain hotels, the Banff Springs was awarded special attention. Beginning in 1902 the original hotel underwent almost continuous expansion until 1912. The first stage involved the allocation of half a million dollars to the duplication of the existing wing, the original and the copy connected by a low wooden passageway.

Walter Painter's pen and ink sketch of his plan for the Banff Springs Hotel, 1906

Reports refer to other "large additions" in 1904 and 1905, probably the beginning of work on the twin towers that were to grace the ends of the wings, and in 1906-07 new laundry, boiler and engine rooms were incorporated. By 1910 company officials had decided to leave this piecemeal approach and build what was essentially a new hotel in place of the old. Given the task of creating this building, which would take until 1928 to complete, was Walter Painter, an American who had been chief architect for the CPR since 1905 and was a disciple of the hotel's original architect, Bruce Price. The hotel he designed has been described as being in the Scottish baronial tradition, itself influenced by the chateaux of the Loire. Painter's first contribution was the eleven-storey concrete centre tower replacing the passageway connecting the two wings. Seventy feet wide and 200 feet long, it was faced with Mount Rundle limestone quarried nearby and installed by Italian stonecutters and Scottish masons. Completed in 1912, the addition allowed the hotel to boast of excellent Turkish baths and two pools, one hot and one cold, that were certain to impress the most discriminating tourists. The same year construction began on a large concrete wing, containing 350 rooms, that Painter had designed for what was soon being referred to as the Chateau Lake Louise, and on a new Hotel Vancouver that he had designed in cooperation with Francis Swales.

The wave of hotel expansion along the CPR line reflected the enormous increase in tourists in the increasingly prosperous years after the turn of the century. The number of passengers carried grew steadily from 4,337,799 in 1901 to 15,480,934 in 1913, and the company was unable to supply enough equipment to meet the demand at certain times. A considerable number of the passengers were tourists; the company's complement of first-class sleeping and dining cars went from 115 in 1901 to almost 400 in 1912. The hotels could not accommodate all comers despite the addition of a large number of rooms. At Glacier House, where the company had taken over the management from H.A. Perley in 1897, there were 1,873 guests in 1902, a figure that jumped to 4,925 after the completion of the new wing. Even with this addition guest space was at a premium and the company placed sleeping cars on a nearby siding to handle the overflow. Mount Stephen House was no better off if the rumours reported by one guest were to be believed: "It has also been whispered, with what truth I cannot say, that as many as four persons have been booked for one room — three being out on little excursions while the fourth was the occupant, *pro tem.*" Most acute were the problems faced by the Banff Springs. In 1902 there were 3,890 guests; as new rooms became available with expansion the numbers climbed to 5,303 in 1903 and 9,684 in 1904. Even with the increase in accommodation it seems that many who came could still not find space, the park superintendent reporting in 1903 that "no less than 5,000 guests were turned away from Banff during the past season" and that "the Banff Springs Hotel was compelled to remain open for a month later than usual owing to its increasing popularity among the travelling public." By 1911 over 22,000 guests were staying at the hotel each summer.

The shortage of hotel accommodation in the mountains was in large part a direct result of the CPR's success in tourist promotion, a success bolstered by the federal government. Railway-government cooperation in developing and promoting the mountain parks had continued after the success of their initial efforts in the eighties and nineties at Banff. Shortly after the turn of the century the government produced the first of a series of its own tourist brochures promoting the parks. *Canadian National Park (Rocky Mountains) Banff, Alberta*, published under the authority of the Minister of the Interior, included all tourist-related information about Rocky Mountains Park and gave CPR facilities high marks, stating that the Banff Springs "commands a view perhaps unrivalled in America" and "ranks

Painter's completed centre tower dramatically changed the original hotel and set the tone for future additions. Byron Harmon photograph

among the finest summer hotels to be found anywhere." But even more important was the government's agreement to provide a certain amount of protection for the company. While the CPR could wield little influence on the development of competing hotels and services in townsites such as Banff and Field, it could, and did, use its influence in more out-of-the-way places. A case in point was Lake Louise, the park superinten-dent stating in a 1910 letter: "The minister has positively refused to allow any more building at Lake Louise. I think he promised Sir Thomas Shaughnessy to that effect and I believe he put up the plea that they wished to have one place in the mountains as nature had left it, except their own hotel accommodation, and the minister has decided that no business of any kind is to be nearer than Lagan [Laggan] station."

Increased mountain tourism brought development of associated services by both the company and private entrepreneurs. The most significant was the transportation service developed by a pioneer Banff family from a small outfitting and guiding concern into North America's largest private sightseeing business, the Brewster Transport Company.

Tom Wilson provided outfitting and guiding services for the CPR in the 1890s, and by the turn of the century he was fulfilling similar needs as well as providing livery services at both Lake Louise and Field. However, in 1904 the CPR chose as "official" outfitters and guides at the Banff Springs the firm of W & J Brewster. Bill and Jim Brewster were twenty-four and twenty-two years old respectively, sons of pioneer Banff dairyman John Brewster, a close friend of Banff Springs manager W.L. Mathews and a prominent Liberal, factors that undoubtedly weighed in the decision. At the time the CPR was operating its own livery service at Banff, having bought out the CPR Transfer Company in 1897, although it was proving to be rather troublesome. Hayter Reed, on taking over as manager-in-chief, quickly decided that such services should be contracted out and in 1905 offered the business to the Brewsters, who jumped at the opportunity to buy the CPR's equipment.

A Brewster sight-seeing tally-ho at the new Banff Springs Hotel Golf Course, 1911

An annual concession fee of $1,500 gave them full use of the CPR's barns and other buildings connected with the livery service and the sole right to solicit conveyance in the Banff Springs Hotel and on the station platform. This agreement gave the Brewsters a tremendous competitive advantage, and with the cooperation of the railway they soon moved to solidify their grip on business at the other CPR hotels in the mountains. In 1908 the contract of Wilson's successor at Lake Louise and Field, Bob Campbell, came up for review; instead of renewing it the Hotel Department awarded it to the Brewsters, leading several noteworthy people in the area to criticize the CPR for its monopolistic tendencies. However, the company argued that dealing with one operator was more practical and efficient. By 1915 the Brewsters had gained complete control of transportation at the mountain hotels with the purchase of the concession at Glacier House from the previous operator. By this time the CPR concessions had helped them to build their company to impressive proportions, with eighty tally-hos, coaches, carriages and wagons, 146 head of driving horses and numerous properties and business interests in Banff. Later they added motorized touring cars and buses, and extended their operations to the CPR's Palliser Hotel in Calgary and eventually as far afield as Hawaii. In time, similar concessions became common at all the CPR's hotels across the country and provided a sound economic base for local tour and transportation operators fortunate enough to acquire them.

Another service, the Lake Louise Tramway, was offered to guests at the Chateau Lake Louise by the CPR itself. Originally Tom Wilson and later the Brewsters had provided service to the hotel by carriage over the rather steep road connecting it with the station at Laggan. However, the grade was hard on horses and in 1911, after hearing from "representatives of societies complaining of cruelty to the animals driven on the road," the government gave permission for the Brewsters to operate motor buses over the route. But the railway had a better solution, building a narrow-gauge tramway for the 3½-mile trip. Beginning in July, 1912, the service used two twenty-eight-foot open-bench passenger cars with internal combustion engines, not unlike the earlier Motor Car used on the main line between Banff and Laggan, each capable of carrying thirty-five passengers, and two freight cars built on similar frames. Operated by

A tramway car stands near the upper station in front of the Rattenbury addition to the Chateau Lake Louise. Byron Harmon photograph

the Hotel Department, the tramway met all regular trains and was forewarned of the arrival of tourist excursion specials by a telephone line linking the hotel and the station. During the height of the summer season the system made up to thirty round trips a day and was in operation until 1930.

The company was, of course, called upon to provide other services and diversions to its hotel guests. At the Banff Springs, in addition to the pools and baths, the company provided indoor entertainments such as billiards and dances two or three nights a week and outdoor activities on its tennis courts and, after 1911, its golf course. At Lake Louise the company supplied Chinese boatmen to propel well-turned-out ladies and gentlemen around the placid waters. Nevertheless it continued to be mountaineering and mountain exploration that attracted the most interest, and the company responded accordingly.

In February, 1906, when the executive heads of the CPR's Western Lines were meeting at Mount Stephen House, A.O. Wheeler, a Dominion Land Surveyor and avid mountaineer, approached William Whyte with a request. Wheeler and fellow enthusiasts had decided that the time had come for Canada to form its own mountaineering club and they were looking for support. He requested twenty CPR passes from any point on the line in Canada to Winnipeg and return so that those interested in a club could gather for a formative meeting. Whyte, recognizing how well the idea fit with the company's tourist program, readily agreed, and the Alpine Club of Canada was created on March 27, 1906, at the Winnipeg YMCA. Since the focus of the club's activities was to be an annual mountaineering camp, to which the participants would travel via the CPR, the company was willing to extend other assistance. The first annual camp was held for 112 members at Yoho Pass in July, 1906, and the CPR provided much of the equipment and personnel necessary to carry it off successfully. Cooks, cook tents and dining canopies came from a CPR camp established in the Yoho Valley and the neophyte alpinists were placed under the care of two of its Swiss guides. Thereafter, as the size of the annual camps grew, it became a matter of course for the company to provide two or more guides.

As for the Swiss guides, close to twenty of them were on the job for various lengths of time between 1899 and 1912. Their services were extended from Glacier House and Mount Stephen House to Lake Louise, where a rustic cabin was built to house them on the lakeshore — a minor project compared with what the CPR developed for the guides farther west.

To spare the expense of providing return passage for the guides to Switzerland each year, passenger traffic manager Robert Kerr suggested in 1909 that the construction of a Swiss Village might provide both a Canadian home for the guides and an interesting attraction for the tourists. He wrote: "For the past three or four years I have been working on an idea for establishing a colony, or Swiss Village, at some point in the mountains — say not farther west than Revelstoke, or in the Columbia Valley on the main line, if a suitable location could be obtained…my idea being somewhere on the slope of a hill, with a southern aspect, in close sight of the main line, to construct a sufficient number of Alpine cottages built after the plan of the little Swiss cottages in the Alps, with a sufficient amount of ground around each cottage where they could grow vegetables, flowers, and keep chickens, goats, etc. — in other words, live just as they live in Switzerland." Kerr saw the colony (he named it Edelweiss) as the climax of the company's "Swiss" campaign. A site was found just to the north of Golden near the main line on a southern slope that "could be easily seen from the train, which generally passed through there in daylight." Six chalets of six rooms each were completed in 1912 and were made available to those of the Swiss guides who were married and had families. This restriction caused problems and, along with the unfulfilled promise of the CPR to provide the Swiss guides with winter work other than some shovelling of snow off the roofs of the hotels, led to discontent in the village. Disillusioned, many of the guides left Edelweiss and it was eventually sold to Edward Feuz's son Walter.

Although it proved rela-

G. Horne Russell's "Moonlight, Fraser Cañon" was included in the CPR's portfolio *Mountain Series B*

tively unsuccessful, Edelweiss was an important example of the CPR's continuing policy of focusing much of its Canadian promotion on the mountains. As in the past, artists and photographers found support for their mountain work, although many of the artists were now commercial illustrators working directly for the company in its advertising program. However, some of the original independent artists still managed to come out and they were joined by a few new, second-generation "railway artists." F.M. Bell-Smith was one of the first group of artists who continued to find inspiration in the Rockies and Selkirks right up to the First World War. Another

CANADIAN ROCKY MOUNTAIN RESORTS

was John Hammond, a Montrealer who had first worked for Notman as a photographer's assistant, accompanying Baltzly as one of the two Notman employees on the 1871 CPR-Geological Survey expedition. After a number of years spent travelling overseas he made several trips to the west in the 1890s and the early 1900s, sometimes accomplishing commissions for the company and its officials. One was a painting of the Governor-General's Coldstream Ranch near Vernon that Van Horne commissioned as a gift to Lord and Lady Aberdeen. Of the newer members of the RCA who became part of the "railway school," perhaps the most successful was G. Horne Russell, who had been primarily a portraitist (Shaughnessy was among his subjects) and a painter of the sea. That he was eventually drawn to the mountains about 1900 may have been related to the fact that he was from Banff, Scotland, and was compelled to see his birthplace's namesake. Russell's paintings often depicted minuscule CPR trains passing through the Kicking Horse or Fraser Canyons where they were dwarfed by the brooding landscape.

Independent photographers, whose numbers were growing in the west, also continued to benefit from periodic CPR passes and sometimes from outright purchase of their photographs for use in promotional literature. One of the most successful was Byron Harmon, a native of Tacoma, Washington, who had established himself at Banff in 1903 and before long stated that his objective was to photograph every peak in the Selkirks and Rockies. Many of his pictures were turned into postcards and by 1907 he was advertising that he could offer the largest selection of Canadian Rockies postcards in existence with "over 100 assorted views." Like other photographers, he attempted to sell his *Along the Line of the Canadian Pacific Railway* series of postcards, viewbooks and enlargements to tourists both on and off the trains. However, the CPR also remained competitive in this field, producing a *Mountain Series B* of its portfolio *Glimpses Along the Canadian Pacific Railway* about 1900, including ten photogravures and two reproductions of paintings, one by G. Horne Russell called "Moonlight, Fraser Cañon." About 1910 all company productions of this type were placed under the responsibility of CPR News Services, the branch of the Passenger Traffic Department responsible for operating newsstands at stations and for the newsagents or "newsies" who sold papers, books, candies and cigarettes on

Lake Louise from C.P.R. Co's Chalet
Lakes in the Clouds Canada
On The Canadian Pacific Railway

Canadian Pacific Railway Company
Dining Car Service

Souvenir packets of menu covers, adorned with high quality photographs, were available to passengers on request

the trains. CPR News Services soon produced its own postcards and viewbooks, many of them reproductions of hand-coloured views, and eventually provided much of the material for such items as promotional pamphlets and menu covers.

The growing pile of promotional literature turned out during these heady times meant that illustrative material, be it art or photograph, was much in demand. Following the success of such productions as *Banff and the Lakes in the Clouds* and *The Challenge of the Mountains* the company began to circulate a brochure featuring its mountain and Pacific coast hotels entitled *Canadian Rocky Mountain Resorts* about 1910. As in past publications, this brochure described the scenery in this section of the line and engineering feats such as the recent Spiral Tunnels, which reduced by half the steep grade on the

infamous Big Hill. However, it was more heavily illustrated than earlier offerings, depicting all the hotels and the attractions in their vicinity, as well as providing information on their services. Joining the hotel brochure was a second new publication, *Pacific Coast Tours Through the Canadian Rockies*, which emphasized the CPR's connections with major Canadian and American cities. Even after a quarter of a century of employing much the same advertising techniques and using the same clichés, the company was still finding them effective and they were once again trotted out for this brochure. Typical of these was the technique of quoting from major publications about the beauties and comforts of the CPR line:

> *The New York* Tribune *says: "It is not generally known that within four days' journey of New York City there are waiting for the sightseer and scientific investigator some of the grandest and most impressive glacial streams in the world. Nothing in Switzerland is to be found more beautiful than the glaciers of the Canadian Rockies and Selkirks, and one of the chief attractions of the trip is the fact that one may journey there and back in civilized luxury, and while enjoying the scenes, at the very 'noses' of the wonderful glaciers themselves, may be comfortable and remain in close touch with the world."*

By this time the inclusion of the mountains in advertising had become such a necessity in the eyes of the company that a follow-up brochure dealing primarily with tours to eastern Canada was issued under the title *Eastern Tours Through The Canadian Pacific Rockies*. This brochure also appears to have been the first to use "Canadian Pacific Rockies" in its title — a slogan that brought Van Horne's old idea of "our mountains" into advertising usage.

The somewhat presumptuous tone of the term "Canadian Pacific Rockies" reflected the confidence of the company as its golden age drew to a close with the onset of the First World War. Its operations had grown enormously over the years from the turn of the century under Shaughnessy's able direction. It had achieved maximum tourist use of its system, now stretching from Liverpool to Hong Kong, and its facilities and equipment were as good as any in the world. It truly was the ultimate fulfillment of the possibilities that Van Horne had envisaged for it on the day the first transcontinental left Montreal. Canada had been taken out of the "backwater" and was now on the "highway," known to tourists the world over.

Group of climbers from the Alpine Club of Canada's annual mountaineering camp at Lake O'Hara in 1909 on Mount Huber. Byron Harmon photograph

Canadian Pacific Steamships Limited became the corporate identity of the company's ocean services in 1921, just prior to its entry into the cruise business

On first glance, many thought the war would be brief and the CPR could even predict profit in the new wartime travel patterns. The European Continent was closed to travel and as the United States had not entered the conflict there would be an increase in the tourist trade in North America. This trend, focused on the widely promoted Panama-Pacific Exposition at San Francisco, turned 1915 into the most successful year yet for tourist travel in Canada. Not until the war had dragged on for several years, involving the United States and sapping the manpower and resources of the western world, would it be recognized as a watershed for many things, including Canadian tourism.

The promotion of North American expositions had become a feature of CPR tourism before the war, the company having profited by excursions to the Chicago World's Fair in 1893 and the Alaska-Yukon-Pacific Exposition in 1909. Gambling on an increase in transcontinental travel, the railway pulled out all the stops for the Panama-Pacific Exposition. A handsome brochure entitled *Pacific Coast Tours...1915* was issued to provide information about the exposition, which was to feature "the manufactures and civilization of the United States and of the World..," although half of it was devoted to promoting tourist stops at the company's facilities in the Rockies on the way to (or from) the exposition. Describing the Canadian Pacific's own exhibit, which was designed by Francis Swales, an English architect who had previously planned the company's pavilion at White City in London, the brochure unabashedly touted the company's position as the pre-eminent railway system in North America:

In a prominent position near the Ferry Slips the Canadian Pacific Railway has erected an attractive Pavilion at the Panama-Pacific Exposition, San Francisco. This illustrates the picturesque character and the natural resources of the country traversed by the railway, and includes among many other things a working model of the Bassano Dam constructed by the Canadian Pacific in Southern Alberta in connection with the greatest irrigation system on the North American Continent. Stretching as it does from the Atlantic to the Pacific, with vast fleets on both Oceans and its hotel and telegraph system, the Canadian Pacific Railway holds a unique position among the railways of this hemisphere, and no one who visits the San Francisco Exposition should fail to pay a visit to this interesting pavilion. Moving pictures illustrating the life and resources of Canada will be displayed in the Pavilion each day during the course of the Exhibition.

The success of the campaign is evident from registrations recorded at the Banff Springs Hotel. During 1915 the total count was 22,019 guests, many of them on conducted tours arranged by large American tour companies such as Raymond & Whitcomb and Gillespie, Kinport & Baird. Private parties included the Governor of New Jersey, the Boston Teachers Club, the American Institute of Architects and the Sons of the American Revolution. The company's concessionaires, Brewster Transport, handled 336 special parties composed of 15,500 people in addition to their ordinary patrons. The increase in American tourists exceeded all expectations. Of the 22,019 guests registered at the hotel, there were 20,276 whose point of origin was known, and of these 17,640 or 87% were Americans. The Atlantic seaboard provided the largest single group, numbering 9,446 or 46%. From New York City alone there were 2,331, just under the total number (2,359) of Canadians visiting the hotel. Overseas tourists had almost disappeared: only 145 from England and the Continent, and 132 from other countries.

The overall tourist flow to Rocky Mountains Park numbered about 90,000, a figure that inspired J.B. Harkin, Commissioner of Dominion Parks, to calculate the monetary yield per acre of scenery in an annual report to the Minister of the Interior:

Publicity experts at the Pacific Coast estimate at $350 the average expenditure of each foreign tourist. But allowing for an expenditure by each foreign visitor to the Rockies of only $250...it is clear that the money brought into Canada by these visitors reaches a very large sum. Take the year 1915, the last year in which owing to war conditions there was a heavy tourist travel from the States. The number of visitors to Rocky Mountains Park in that year was approximately 90,000. Over 65,000 of these visitors were foreigners. Allowing for an expenditure of $250 each it follows that over $16,000,000 of foreign money was brought into Canada by

The CPR pavilion at the 1915 Panama-Pacific Exposition designed by Francis Swales

people of other countries who were attracted to this park...
Now it is interesting to compare the value on an acreage basis
of our exports of wheat with what we may call our exports in
scenery. The acreage of Rocky Mountains Park in 1915 was
1,800 square miles, or 1,152,000 acres, and the value of the
foreign tourist traffic it attracted was roughly speaking
$16,000,000. This works out to a per acreage value of $13.88.

The total wheat exports for the same year were valued...at
$74,293,548. The number of acres under wheat cultivation in
all Canada were 15,109,415, which means that the value of
our wheat exported that year was equivalent to $4.91 per acre.
That is, our export of scenery per acre in Rocky Mountains
Park was equal to almost three times the acreage value of our
exportable wheat surplus.

This does not take into account the money which was kept
in Canada by the 24,000 Canadians who took their holidays
in the parks in that year and which would add another
$2,000,000 or $3,000,000 to the total.

Thus Harkin reckoned Van Horne's policy of "capitalizing the scenery" in dollars and cents and committed federal funds to a promotion campaign that nicely complemented the CPR's own tourist efforts.

The man mainly responsible for the company's successful tourist campaign in connection with the Panama-Pacific Exposition was its general publicity agent, John Murray Gibbon. In 1913 Shaughnessy again attached George Ham directly to his own office, to function as a political lobbyist for the company, and brought Gibbon from London to replace Ham in the publicity office. The president changed the title of the position from advertising agent to general publicity agent to cover the dual responsibilities of advertising and public relations, and had Gibbon report directly to the vice-president of traffic, G.M. Bosworth. At the same time Shaughnessy created the position of general tourist agent to ensure that tourist information was distributed to travel bureaux and company agents and to answer the numerous enquiries from sportsmen and vacationists. Its first occupant, A.O. Seymour, worked with Gibbon to coordinate tourist facilities and services with tourist advertising.

In 1946 at a banquet held in his honour by the Canadian Authors' Association, of which he was the founder and first president, Gibbon would be hailed as a nation builder. As a publicity man he would project an extremely positive image for the CPR in the years after the First World War in the eyes of

John Murray Gibbon, pictured at Lake McArthur during a Sky Line Hike. Nicholas Morant photograph

both Canadians and foreign tourists alike. He did it by promoting the cultural traditions and abilities of the diverse racial groups in the country, by fostering the skills of its artists, musicians, craftsmen and authors, and by making the country's history and traditions something to be proud of rather than forgotten or suppressed. CPR management was not always aware of what he was doing; Gibbon used the influence and freedom of his position to forward his own interests, which he saw as being one and the same with the interests of both the company and the country In a way, he was a successor to Van Horne, who had patronized Canadian artists and photographers in the course of producing the first CPR tourist brochures. But for Gibbon, CPR promotion was merely a vehicle for his personal campaign to discover and support Canadian culture.

Gibbon set the tone for his new job as general publicity agent when Shaughnessy requested proposals for extending the influence of the company's advertising campaign in Canada. Gibbon's response was an unequivocal call to involve French-Canadians in the process. Pointing out that George Ham had cultivated the editors of English-language newspapers, but not the French-language press, Gibbon suggested that the French-Canadian editors be asked to nominate an assistant for the CPR's publicity office. The ploy worked and Raoul Clouthier, a young journalist, was put forward for the job. Later, when Ham became ill and unable to carry on his duties, Gibbon suggested that the Toronto editors, suspicious of the CPR because of its Montreal base, be given the same option. They nominated J. Harry Smith, financial editor of the Montreal *Gazette*, who in 1922 became the manager of the new Canadian Pacific Press Bureau, with Clouthier heading the French section. This commitment to involving French-Canadians led to the production of French-language promotional material, and brochures, pamphlets and posters were issued in both

English and French throughout the twenties.

Much of Gibbon's attention in his first few years as general publicity agent was directed to the war effort. The CPR made an enormous commitment of ships, personnel, facilities and material towards winning the war and consequently suffered to some degree because of it. Tourism inevitably declined. There were no overseas customers, and few from the United States after it joined the conflict in 1917. A huge segment of Canadian manpower had been sent overseas to fight and most Canadians remaining at home devoted themselves entirely to winning the war. Passenger traffic declined only marginally, from 15,648,312 in 1914 to 14,396,753 in 1918, but most of the passengers during the war were military personnel. Over the same period, the number of first-class sleeping and dining cars declined from a record high of 502 to 480. Most enlightening are the statistics for the Banff Springs Hotel, where the number of guests slipped from a high of 22,019 in 1915 to just 9,414 in 1917. Wartime declines were accepted with equanimity. But the anticipated postwar recovery failed to materialize, and 1921 passenger figures stood at 15,318,358, almost exactly the same as in 1914, and Banff Springs registrations at 12,979, far below the 1915 record.

Shaughnessy had been faced with failing eyesight during the

The *Empress of France* at Batavia, Java on its 1925 round-the-world cruise

war and in 1918, like Van Horne before him, had decided to leave the presidency and serve as chairman. The new president was Edward Wentworth Beatty, who had grown up with the company as a son of Henry Beatty, first manager of the CPR's Great Lakes steamers. But he had a much different background from his predecessors. Beatty graduated from the University of Toronto in law and joined the CPR's Law Department in 1901. Gibbon had got on well with Shaughnessy, an avid reader of novels who, after reading Gibbon's first novel *Hearts and Faces* in 1916, summoned the author to his office and awarded him a $100-a-month increase in salary. Beatty, a man educated in the arts and later chancellor of McGill University, was even more receptive to Gibbon's view of the company's role in promoting culture, although he was sometimes kept in the dark as to his general publicity agent's activities.

Beatty's first target in postwar reconstruction was the company's steamship services, a not surprising choice given his family background and the fact that these services had suffered most severely in the war. The company had lost thirteen ships by sinking, two of them new Atlantic passenger liners, two by accident and eight through purchase by the Royal Navy. Others such as the *Empress of Asia* and the *Empress of Russia* of the Pacific fleet had been fitted out as armed merchant cruisers and troopships, substantially depreciating their value. During the war the two separate steamship operations run by the company, the CPR's own and the Allan Line, were amalgamated into Canadian Pacific Ocean Services, a name changed to Canadian Pacific Steamships Limited in 1921. This new corporate entity added four Clyde-built ships, three for the Atlantic and one for the Pacific. These were two-class ships, third-class and cabin-class. Shaughnessy had introduced cabin-class accommodation to CPR ships just before the war, correctly foreseeing an increasing market for a less elaborate but comfortable passage for an increasingly travel-conscious middle class. Also, through the Reparations Commission, purchases of German liners were made, the most important being those ships that became the *Empress of Scotland* and the *Empress of Australia*.

The company developed a new tourist scheme to make full use of its new and enlarged fleet — the cruise. The first of the CPR cruises took place in 1922 when the Frank C. Clark Travel Agency of New York chartered the *Empress of Scotland* and the *Empress of France* for seventy-four-day cruises to the Mediterranean. The Clark company chartered the same liners again the following year, the *Empress of France* for a round-the-world cruise and the *Empress of Scotland* for a Mediterranean cruise. Meanwhile, Canadian Pacific Steamships, noting the success of the first Clark cruises, organized two of its own twenty-seven-day cruises to the West Indies in 1922. Beginning in 1924 the company operated all its own cruises, including annual round-the-world cruises and cruises to the West Indies, the Spanish Main and the Mediterranean. The advertising for the round-the-world voyage of the *Empress of France* leaving New York on January 14 and returning May 23, 1925, provides a typical example of CPR cruise promotion:

There may arise in the minds of those seriously considering going round the world the question, "Should we join a Cruise or travel independently, making our own arrangements from port to port?"

While the Canadian Pacific has excellent facilities for independent travel round the world, there are so many attractive features about a Cruise that it is easy to decide. Every detail for your comfort and entertainment is arranged months in advance by experts who know every angle of cruising.

From the moment you go on board, the Empress of France is your home for the entire trip. You can put your clothes away in your stateroom and send your empty trunks to the baggage room. There is no continual packing and unpacking on a Cruise — just the few articles required for the excursions on shore.

There are no hotel or train reservations for you to worry about, as everything has been attended to.

You also avoid the discomforts of having to travel on small local steamers, to say nothing of the delays frequently experienced as a result of their uncertain departures.

Our arrangements for sight-seeing in high-class motor cars are ideal and you are not at the mercy of unscrupulous drivers. Furthermore, you see everything that is worth seeing and no time is wasted on unimportant places.

Then there is that congenial companionship and those delightful friendships which predominate on a Cruise. Everyone is carefree and happy, and when it comes to the end of the Cruise, you reluctantly say good bye, wishing in your heart that you were just starting out.

Advertising stressed the great escape from winter:

The enjoyment of a cruise largely depends on visiting the various countries at the right season for sight-seeing, thus avoiding extreme heat and cold. A close study of the itinerary on page eight will show first, that we are departing from the winter of this country as soon as practicable after New Year's, then a succession of springtimes — the Mediterranean ports at the height of the Riviera season; Palestine before the heat and dust; Egypt, when it is gayest; India, well before the hot season; China, in its springtime; Japan, at the famous cherry blossom season; Hawaii and British Columbia at a good time; and back to California early in May and New York before the end of May. It will be springtime at home and you will have escaped those many disagreeable storms of January to April, while enjoying delightful weather cruising.

Because of the success of its first cruises, Canadian Pacific Steamships quickly expanded its advertising campaign. Some of the most exquisite and expensive promotional pamphlets ever produced anywhere, for anything, were issued for various CPR cruises from the mid- to the late twenties. Colour in every hue of the rainbow was combined with gold and silver leaf to enrich the exotic flavour of the scenes depicted by the talented illustrators. The slogan-conscious company added its most imaginative catch-phrase on record to support its campaign — "See this World before the Next by The World's Greatest Travel System." Over the next fifty years the company would operate more than 500 cruises.

Back in postwar Canada the CPR faced a basic change in transportation — the automobile. By the twenties automobiles had become affordable to the average man and a skeletal system of roads had been built in Canada. North American tourism was quickly democratized as the means became available to reach holiday destinations previously reserved for middle- and upper-class railroad travellers, who were themselves turning to the automobile as a novel and versatile way to see the Canadian landscape. The initial effects were local or regional in nature, long-distance motor travel being a few years in the future. From the CPR's point of view the automobile could mean an increase in guests at its hotels in eastern Canada, while reducing short-haul traffic. In 1920, when 93,000 cars entered Canada from the United States, Montreal, the Maritimes, and resorts on the St. Lawrence and in the Muskoka and Georgian Bay districts registered record tourist business.

The opening of the Banff-Windermere Highway through Sinclair Canyon in 1923 unlocked the potential of the mountains for automobile tourists from the Canadian and American Pacific coasts. Byron Harmon photograph

It was in the mountains, at the heart of CPR tourist promotion, that the automobile problem was acute. Because of a lack of roads and a government ban on cars in the national parks, the CPR's mountain business had been almost completely insulated from the effects of the automobile in the prewar period. But by war's end the prohibition had ended and the government had embarked on an ambitious program of linking Rocky Mountains Park with the outside world. The CPR could tolerate local or regional road connections — the long-distance tourist would still have to travel by rail — but road systems linking Canada and the United States would spell disaster. Among the proponents of the new roads was J.B. Harkin, who had painstakingly calculated the per acre tourist dollar value of the parks in 1915. Using a similar formula he computed that the value of the 93,000 cars entering Canada from the United States had amounted to over $16,000,000: Canada's total tourist revenue for the year was $75,000,000. A connecting road system had actually been under construction for several years as a result of a joint federal, British Columbia and Alberta government agreement to build the Banff-Windermere Highway through the Vermilion Pass.

Because of British Columbia's delay in completing its section of the road a new inter-governmental agreement had to be worked out in 1919. The federal government promised to complete the B.C. section in return for 600 square miles of land along the route; this would form the new Kootenay National Park. The road officially opened in June, 1923, unlocking the automobile tourist potential of the western United States and the west coast of Canada. Connections from Invermere, B.C., could be made via Cranbrook to Spokane, Seattle, Vancouver, Victoria, Portland, San Francisco and Los Angeles. This western section of what became known as the Grand Circle Tour was complemented by an eastern section, which led from California to the Grand Canyon, then north via Salt Lake City and Yellowstone and Glacier National Parks, crossing the border at Coutts, Alberta, and proceeding to Macleod and Calgary.

Long before the Banff-Windermere Highway was completed, the CPR's Hotel Department had responded to the challenge of the automobile by simply adding it to its tourist services. In conjunction with its concessionaire, Brewster Transport, the company organized a series of "Twenty-Four-Hour Motor Detour Tours" to allow tourists detraining at Banff to spend a day touring the Rockies in a fleet of Packard touring cars and White buses, stay the night at the Chateau Lake Louise, and drive to Golden to board a westbound train the next day. Several other motor detour options were added and by the late twenties the CPR and the Great Northern Railway had worked out an excursion plan allowing an interchange of passengers by automobile between Glacier Park in Montana and Banff.

The company also began adjusting hotel facilities to meet demands of motorists after the war. Hayter Reed had retired as manager-in-chief of hotels in 1915 and was succeeded by Frank L. Hutchinson, another former manager of the Chateau Frontenac who became Reed's assistant in 1911 and superintendent of hotels for Alberta and British Columbia in 1912. Working with him as superintendent of construction and maintenance, Western Lines, was Basil Gardom, an innovative individual who had begun his career with the company as the manager of its tramway operation at Lake Louise. In addition to its Emerald Lake Chalet, the CPR opened basic tourist camps at Moraine Lake and in the Yoho Valley in 1906. Gardom expanded these into bungalow camps and added new camps at other locations, believing the postwar CPR guest would prefer to stay in smaller, quieter and less expensive accommodation than the company's major mountain hotels. Gardom's first new mountain bungalow camp was built in 1921 at Wapta Lake in the Kicking Horse Pass, accessible by road to both Field and Emerald Lake. It was followed the next year by two similar camps, the Lake O'Hara Camp built on the shore of the beautiful lake over Abbot Pass from Lake Louise, and the Yoho Valley Camp built at the foot of the magnificent Takakkaw Falls. The company issued individual brochures to promote these camps:

YOHO VALLEY BUNGALOW CAMP

Facing Takakkaw Falls, in the beautiful Yoho Valley. One and two room bungalows, with central dining and recreation room. Total accommodation, 36 guests. Open from July 1st to September 15th. Reached from Field (11 miles) or from Hector (13 miles) — in each case by automobile. Postal address, Yoho Valley Camp, Field, B.C. Rates — $5.50 per day, $35.00 per week, American Plan.

An ideal centre for hiking, pony trips and mountain climbing.

YOHO VALLEY
Bungalow Camp

Canadian Pacific Rockies

The bungalow camp concept was immediately successful and the company extended the facilities to the Banff-Windermere Highway as it neared completion. A bungalow camp had been built on the shore of Lake Windermere in 1920 and several more were added at convenient locations along the road to Banff; the Castle Mountain (later Storm Mountain) and Vermilion River Bungalow Camps opened in 1923 and the

Radium Hot Springs Bungalow Camp in 1926. Supplementing the company's camps was a system of teahouses and resthouses to serve the needs of trail riders, hikers and motorists. Such units were constructed on the Saddleback above Lake Louise and at Summit Lake above the Yoho Valley in 1922; at Twin Falls in the Yoho Valley, Lake Agnes near Lake Louise and the Nakimu Caves in Glacier Park in 1923; the Plain of Six Glaciers near the foot of Mount Victoria and in the Kicking Horse Canyon in 1924; and at the Natural Bridge on the Kicking Horse River in 1925. In 1922 the company built what was probably meant to be the first of a number of high-altitude mountaineering huts near Abbot Pass, but this initiative was never followed up. The company extended the camp concept to hunters and fishermen in Ontario in 1923, building facilities at French River and Nipigon River.

As the Hotel Department developed the bungalow camp and teahouse network, two of the first three hotels built by the CPR disappeared from the system. In 1918 Mount Stephen House was turned over to the railway branch of the YMCA, the first step in a plan for a new, more modern hotel in the area. This plan was abandoned after construction of the nearby Lake Wapta Camp and enlargement of the Emerald Lake Chalet. At Glacier the hotel had been cut off from the line when the CPR completed the five-mile-long Connaught Tunnel in 1916 to reduce the grade in the Rogers Pass section. The company continued to operate Glacier House after the war, hoping that a proposed road linking Golden and Revelstoke would re-establish it in main-line travel. In 1925 the foundations for an addition were laid but at the end of the season the hotel was abruptly closed. It was demolished in 1929, a year after the government decided to build its road along the Big Bend, far to the north of Glacier House.

No climber himself, John Murray Gibbon saw to it that sufficient literature was published to maintain the flow of mountaineers to the CPR hotels and camps. The most elaborate of these publications was *Easy Climbs in the Canadian Pacific Rockies*, a handsome thirty-two-page brochure illustrated with photographs, mostly from the collection of Banff mountain photographer Byron Harmon. It was aimed at neophyte alpinists, providing information about equipment, the availability of Swiss guides and other company services in the mountains. A companion piece soon appeared, authored by

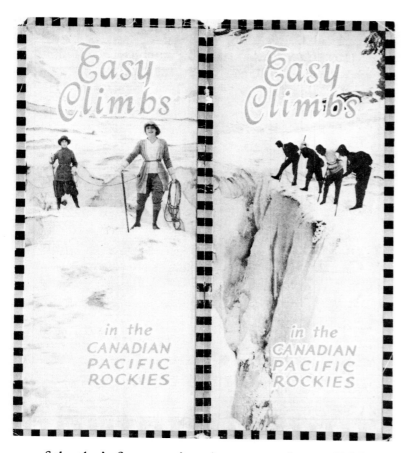

one of the day's foremost American mountaineers, Val Fynn, entitled *What to Wear Walking, Riding, Climbing and Big Game Hunting in the Canadian Pacific Rockies.*

If Gibbon was none too adept at mountaineering, such was not the case with trail riding and hiking, and into these two pursuits he put much of his own and the company's energies. Before the war, outfitting and guiding had been a major factor in the economy of the national parks with parties of mountaineers, hunters, scientists and tourist-explorers travelling by horseback to the farthest reaches of the mountain wilderness. After the war this activity languished, as the tourists indulged their love affair with the automobile. Gibbon, although primarily interested in writing and the arts, was also a great believer in the healthful benefits of outdoor activities and had been an enthusiastic horseman since 1909 when, during one of his summer visits to Canada, he had taken his first trail ride into the Yoho Valley under the guidance of Tom Wilson. Numerous other rides had followed as he was able to fit them into his summer schedule and since "it also fitted in with my growing

habit of song-writing. To lie in a teepee beside the fire, resting on a mattress lined with eiderdown and supported on a layer of pine boughs, seemed to create an ideal atmosphere for the conception of a song, particularly a song of the outdoors in the mountains." In 1923 he accompanied a CPR-sponsored party of fishermen, which included H.B. Clow, president of Rand McNally mapmakers, Reginald Townsend, editor of *Country Life in America*, R.H. Palenske, a noted Chicago artist, and Byron Harmon of Banff, on a trail trip to the upper Kootenay River area. While camped on the Wolverine Plateau the party was beset by a blizzard and during several days of layover the talk centred on the subject of trailriding. Gibbon came up with the idea of forming an order of riders that would issue buttons of various grades to those riding fifty, one hundred, five hundred, one thousand and two thousand five hundred miles of mountain trails. Those present agreed and since Gibbon claimed he could get the support of the CPR for what they decided to call the Trail Riders of the Canadian Rockies, he was appointed secretary-treasurer in charge of promotion.

The Trail Riders, like the Alpine Club of Canada, yielded obvious benefits for CPR tourism. The organization would hold an annual trail ride in the mountains, beginning and ending at some point near the company's hotels or bungalow camps. The riders would take the train to the mountains and bunk with the CPR after camping out on the trail. To attract the "right" people, Gibbon ensured that the executive was made up of prominent names, among them the honorary president, Charles D. Walcott, Secretary of the Smithsonian Institution, and council members J.B. Harkin, Commissioner of Dominion Parks, W.T. Hornaday, Director of the New York Zoological Society, Sir James Outram, the conqueror of Mount Assiniboine, and Carl Rungius, the wildlife artist. He was also eager to have notables qualify for membership and mileage buttons, a fact evident in a letter to Jim Brewster in August, 1923: "If you have anything to do with the Prince of Wales when he comes out, you might see that he rides at least fifty miles, so as to qualify for membership. It would help quite a bit if we could rope him in."

The first annual trail ride began at Yoho Valley Camp in July, 1924, and Gibbon launched it with a tribute to the pioneer trail rider of the Canadian Rockies, Tom Wilson. He commissioned a leading French-Canadian sculptor, Henri Hébert, to design and cast a bronze plaque honouring Wilson as the discoverer of Lake Louise and Emerald Lake. Before the 207 riders started off the plaque was unveiled after a speech by Mary Vaux (now Mrs. Charles D. Walcott), a song by Frances James, a soloist from the Banff Springs Hotel, and a brief reply by Wilson, who claimed that "I am not accustomed to extemporaneous speaking unless a cayuse has stepped upon my foot." By honouring Wilson, Gibbon created an "historic person" who could be featured in CPR advertising. From 1927 until his death in 1933 Wilson was employed at the Banff Springs Hotel and Chateau Lake Louise as local colour, entertaining tourists and newspaper reporters with stories drawn from his vast repertoire of trail lore.

The Trail Riders of the Canadian Rockies proved more successful than Gibbon had dared hope. At the conclusion of each ride a Pow-wow was held in a large tent erected near one of

the company's lodgings. Harold Eustace Key, musical director of the Hotel Department, brought a portable harmonium and acted as song leader and Wilf Carter, an aspiring cowboy singer, was recruited as an entertainer. By 1929 the order could count some 1,500 names in its membership, and subsidiary rides, also using CPR accommodation, were organized.

Gibbon later discovered many people — the CPR president, Edward Beatty, among them — liked the idea of an outing, but preferred to walk rather than ride. This led to the creation of a sister order in 1933, the Sky Line Trail Hikers of the Canadian Rockies, with Beatty as its honorary president. It held an annual outing in the form of a hike and Gibbon, acting as its secretary-treasurer as well, was able to attract many new people to the mountain trails. In Gibbon's view, the main benefit of both organizations was the good feeling they engendered between American visitors and the Canadians with whom they shared the campfire.

The automobile was not the only competitor challenging the CPR's hold on Canadian tourist business after the war. There was a new challenge in the railroad business with completion of two rival lines, the Canadian Northern and the Grand Trunk Pacific, and their subsequent nationalization into the government-operated Canadian National Railways, a process completed in 1922. The company had been accustomed to competition for tourist business in the east, particularly from the venerable Grand Trunk Railway, but competition in the west was something new. The lines forming Canadian National Railways had borrowed many ideas from the CPR in their own tourist promotion: the Canadian Northern brought out artists, including A.Y. Jackson and J.W. Beatty, to paint in the mountains as early as 1914; and the Grand Trunk Pacific became involved in the development of Jasper Park Lodge in 1921. This competition for the mountain tourist developed into a battle between Banff on the CPR in the south and Jasper on the

The competition between the CPR in the south and the Grand Trunk Pacific in the north was exemplified in the advertising section of the 1915 *Canadian Alpine Journal*.

CNR in the north. It was a battle that the CPR was determined to win, as indicated by the huge amount of high-quality advertising material the company turned out in the twenties.

The CPR's advertising literature of the twenties differed in two main respects from that of the prewar period; it was more elaborate in its format and it made extensive use of colour. Rather than the typical pocket-sized accordion-folded pamphlet, the new brochures were large and unfolded, to accommodate (without creases) the beautiful illustrations adorning their pages. They often contained dozens of photographs, and detailed information replaced the testimonials and scenic description of earlier material. The large quantity of art reproduction in them emanated from Gibbon's close relationship with numerous Canadian and foreign artists and from the company's policy, developed in its cruise advertising, of attracting patrons with the imaginative use of colour. The company's relationship with artists therefore operated at several levels in this period.

As in the past, members of the RCA came to paint the mountains with the assistance of the company. Charles W. Simpson, one of Quebec's foremost landscape painters, was in the mountains on several occasions and his paintings were often used for full-colour illustrations. American artists such as Carl Rungius and R.H. Palenske also visited the mountains annually and both had some of their work reproduced. The two, like Simpson, were friends of Gibbon and he was able to ensure free transportation and other CPR perks for them. Rungius was the foremost wildlife painter in North America and some of the most magnificent CPR illustrations ever produced appeared from his work in various editions of *Resorts in the Canadian Rockies*. Palenske excelled as a commercial illustrator and he provided attractive colour renderings of interiors and events, previously illustrated with black-and-white photographs. He was commissioned to execute a series of watercolour paintings to illustrate individual brochures on the Banff Springs Hotel and the Chateau Lake Louise, reflecting the gaiety, luxury and elegance that was so much a part of their appeal in the twenties.

A number of artists worked directly for the CPR but achieved recognition beyond the limits of commercial art. A good example was A.C. Leighton, a young Sussex-born artist who in 1924 came to the attention of the CPR's London office by constructing a working scale model of the port of Liverpool. He was hired by the company as an illustrator for its cruise campaign, and in 1925 with Leonard Richman, another company artist, he visited Canada and became fascinated by the mountains. The company had first choice of his work from his Canadian trips, leaving Leighton to sell the rest for his own profit. Leighton continued to work in London for the CPR until 1929, when his mountain paintings earned him appointment as art director at the Art Institute in Calgary. Soon afterwards he organized the Alberta Society of Artists and went on to become one of the founders of the Banff School of Fine Arts. He was one of the west's finest landscape painters.

Photographs for CPR brochures came from independent photographers, from the company's official photographer, J.C.S. Bennett, and, as the twenties progressed, from a new agency called Associated Screen News. From the time Beatty had become president he was interested in the possibilities of using motion pictures to promote tourism. Approached by American interests about sharing in the development of a newsreel plant on Long Island, he turned to Gibbon for advice. Gibbon recommended the company pursue the idea only if the Americans agreed that there should be a Canadian branch to produce motion pictures on Canadian subjects. He also recommended that B.E. Norrish, head of the Canadian government's photographic department, be approached to head the branch. In 1920 Associated Screen News was formed in Montreal with Norrish as managing director. The new agency accomplished its objectives very successfully with motion pictures promoting travel in Canada soon becoming widely available.

Gibbon contributed substantially to the postwar tourist campaign that won the war of the mountain west for the CPR, but he left his mark by promoting Canadian culture as a tourist attraction to fill CPR hotels across the country in the spring and fall "shoulder" seasons. In 1926 Gibbon was called on to publicize the opening of a new wing of the Chateau Frontenac.

North American Alps
Canadian Rockies

MOUNT ROBSON ROUTE

S THE STEEL OF THE GRAND TRUNK CIFIC has penetrated the Canadian Rocky Mountain Range, through the Yellowhead Pass, the Railway opened up one of the most interesting territories on American Continent, from a scenic standpoint as well from the Alpine climbers' view.

One hundred miles of continuous mountain scenery, h gigantic peaks rising on all sides to heights of from ht thousand to fourteen thousand feet, are offered to ose who desire new fields to explore. Great mountains are on every hand, but above all stands Mount obson, "a giant amongst giants and immeasurably preme".

A handsome publication entitled "The North American Alps" embodying most interesting data regarding the new egion, has been issued by the Grand Trunk Pacific Railway, and copies may be had free for the asking. Write for a copy.

G. T. BELL   W. P. HINTON   W. E. DUPEROW
Passenger Traffic   Asst. Passenger Traffic   Asst. General
Manager   Manager   Passenger Agent
MONTREAL   MONTREAL   WINNIPEG

The Rev. Charles Gordon preaching the service at the Banff Highland Gathering, 1928

He came up with a plan to hold a dinner for newspaper editors from Montreal, Toronto and the United States, with entertainment in the form of folksongs demonstrating the traditional background of the people of Quebec. This event proved so popular that Gibbon's English translations of the songs performed at the dinner were quickly published by J.M. Dent and Sons under the title of *Canadian Folksongs Old and New*. It encouraged him to plan another festival the following year when the manager-in-chief of hotels asked him to provide a spring attraction for the Chateau Frontenac. The first of the annual Folksong and Handicraft Festivals at the hotel lasted four days and consisted of traditional French-Canadian folksinging, dancing accompanied by country fiddlers and an exhibition of the skills of Quebec weavers and spinners. To help assemble the handicraft exhibit he enlisted the support of the Canadian Handicraft Guild, the furriers Holt Renfrew, the Quebec government and the National Museum of Canada. Attendance was so heavy that many of those wishing to see one of the performances at the Chateau Frontenac were turned away.

When Gibbon was given the task of filling the Banff Springs Hotel at Labour Day, 1927, the way he had filled the Chateau Frontenac in the spring of 1926, he suggested a Highland Gathering and Scottish Music Festival. The Hotel Department agreed and Beatty himself was persuaded to offer a silver cup to the winner of a competition of regimental pipers. Other attractions included Scottish folksingers, a Hebridean choir singing Gaelic songs, a Highland dance competition and an open-air sermon in dress kilt by the Rev. Charles W. Gordon, a popular author who wrote under the pen name of Ralph Connor. Like the Quebec festival, the Highland Gathering proved tremendously successful and, in a letter of appreciation to Beatty, Gordon paid tribute to Gibbon's work: "The unseen moving and directing spirit behind it all deserves the full credit for perfect arrangement of detail, for harmonious cooperation of all the artists, but very specially for the conception of the whole festival as a united thing. To my mind Mr. Murray Gibbon has achieved a notable thing in Canada, and has initiated a thing that will not die."

The festival idea was quickly expanded. For the Quebec festival Beatty offered a prize of $3,000 for the best composition based on a French-Canadian melody and the Governor-General, Lord Willingdon, offered to act as patron. Beatty suggested that Gibbon should arrange other festivals at the company's hotels in the west to create better understanding between ethnic groups. Gibbon responded with the New Canadian Festival, first held at the Royal Alexandra Hotel in Winnipeg in June, 1928, with four hundred performers representing fifteen groups. Other festivals followed: the Great West Canadian Folksong, Folkdance and Handicrafts Festivals held at the Hotel Saskatchewan in Regina and the Palliser Hotel in Calgary, which included Scottish, Irish and Welsh representation as well as seventeen other groups; a Sea Music Festival at the Hotel Vancouver featuring music from Canada's Atlantic and Pacific coasts; and an English Music Festival held in conjunction with the opening of the company's magnificent Royal York Hotel, the largest in the Commonwealth, in Toronto in 1929.

Gibbon's folk festivals survived the Depression, when appropriations for all advertising and promotion were pared to the bone. However, when Canadian Pacific Telegraphs entered the radio field in the early thirties they were incorporated into radio broadcasts and discontinued as staged events. Gibbon himself became involved in broadcasting, doing a program called "Canadian Mosaic" based on his research into Canada's ethnic and racial groups for the festivals. This material later appeared in his book *Canadian Mosaic*, an important contribution to Canada's social history and a winner of the Governor-General's Award in 1938.

Gibbon's festivals proved to be highly beneficial for both the CPR and the country, graphically illustrating the significance of CPR tourist promotion in Canadian culture. Perhaps the best assessment came from B.K. Sandwell, the Toronto man of letters, in his citation during the ceremony at which Gibbon received the Lorne Pierce Gold Medal of the Royal Society of Canada in 1949:

When he came to this country in 1913, Dr. Gibbon immediately realized that in the arts, and especially the traditional and folk arts, of her people, Canada possessed resources which she was grievously failing to exploit, and almost completely failing to encourage.

Only those who can recall the manner in which these traditional arts were ignored by the "cultural" elements of the country before the First World War can realize the extent of the revolution which was started by Dr. Gibbon when he set himself to make them an important and essential part of the picture of Canada as envisaged by the world at large. Today

they are universally accepted as foreground material in that picture, but the change which has happened in a single generation is largely the result of the discernment, courage and tenacity of this one man — backed up, it must be admitted, by the farseeing directors of a great transportation system...

I cannot omit reference to the fact that he early discovered the immense riches of French Canada in this field of folk and traditional arts and that by making them better known to the English-speaking world he contributed powerfully to that mutual understanding between peoples of the two languages in Canada...

CZECHO-SLOVAKIA

GREAT WEST CANADIAN

FOLKSONG AND HANDICRAFTS
FOLKDANCE FESTIVAL

REGINA, MARCH, 20-23-1929

*Illustrating the wealth of Art and Music --
-- brought to CANADA by recent settlers from Europe*

SINGERS, INSTRUMENTALISTS, FOLK-DANCERS | HANDICRAFTS ORGANIZED BY THE CANADIAN HANDICRAFTS GUILD;
FROM 20 RACIAL GROUPS IN PICTURESQUE | MUSIC AND FOLK-DANCING ORGANIZED BY THE
COSTUMES OF THEIR COUNTRY OF ORIGIN: | CANADIAN PACIFIC RAILWAY.

For illustrated pamphlet and reservations apply-local CANADIAN PACIFIC agents or-

HOTEL SASKATCHEWAN, REGINA

This composite photograph and painting depicts the typical make-up of an early transcontinental passenger train. Notman composite

Portfolio

Professor O. B. Buell was an accomplished photographer who, with the company's assistance, captured aspects of life along the line. This view, probably taken in 1884, he captioned "Bow River, Indian washing." O. B. Buell photograph

"A Cree family and travois ready for a journey" illustrates the quality of the reproductions in the CPR's portfolio *Indian Series A,* available to tourists for purchase

Despite operating under adverse conditions, Benjamin Baltzly, working for William Notman on a CPR contract, returned from the west in 1871 with some fine views.
Benjamin Baltzly photograph

William McFarlane Notman's 1884 views had proven so useful to Canadian Pacific that he and his brother Charles were provided with a photographer's car (behind the locomotive), complete with a darkroom, in 1887 and 1889. Notman photograph

Notman's mammoth plate views taken in 1887 and 1889 provided high-quality images in a large format (45.7 x 55.9 cm.) In this view taken at Banff's Upper Hot Springs one of the Notmans and his mammoth plate camera have become a part of the photograph in the right foreground. Notman photograph

Ideas about the preservation of nature were balanced by sportsmen's interests in exploiting the fish and game to be found in the wilderness of North America

Nature in a tamer form, Vancouver's new Stanley Park, was destined to become one of the prime tourist attractions of the CPR's western terminus. Notman photograph

Alexander Henderson's photographs were sensitive portraits of the mountain landscape. This view, entitled "In Beaver River Valley Near 6-Mile Creek, CPR, B.C.," is one of the few surviving photographs of his 1885 trip. Alexander Henderson photograph

Boorne and May were two of the most successful commercial photographers plying their trade along the line between Calgary and the Pacific coast. Boorne and May photograph

Tourists from around the world were provided with the opportunity to form friendships both on the train and at stopover points such as Glacier House. Vaux family photograph

An around-the-world tour on the company's *Empresses* and P. & O. liners was a time of relaxation and enjoyment for well-heeled passengers

The Canadian government published its first major piece of tourist literature to support the efforts of Canadian Pacific in 1904

An advertising poster for the CPR's Great Lakes steamers prior to the completion of the transcontinental line

The CPR's famous Red Letter Day poster advertising the initiation of transcontinental service

The Challenge of the Mountains, produced shortly after the turn of the century, was the first company brochure to feature a full colour cover

John Fraser's "The Rogers Pass" may have been one of the paintings commissioned by George Stephen for the Colonial and Indian Exhibition. "The Rogers Pass," John Fraser, 1886, oil on canvas, 55.9 x 76.2 cm.

Lucius O'Brien, as the first president of the R.C.A., was the foremost Canadian artist of the day and, with the aid of CPR passes, was able to paint extensively in the mountain west. "Gate of the Canyon," Lucius O'Brien, 1888, watercolour over graphite on wove paper, 47.1 x 67.3 cm.

"Cloud Capped Towers," (Mt. Sir Donald,) Lucius O'Brien, 1886, watercolour, 77.5 x 57.5 cm.

Thomas Mower Martin was one of the day's popular watercolourists who frequently travelled west on Canadian Pacific passes. "Landscape with a Boat," T. Mower Martin, 1887, watercolour, 52 x 33.7 cm.

George Horne Russell, one of the second wave of railway artists to paint the mountain west, was noted for his dark, brooding landscapes with miniscule trains. "Kicking Horse Pass," G. Horne Russell, 1900, oil on canvas, 197.5 x 150.5 cm.

Peter Whyte was the first native Banff artist to paint aspects of the scenery and the company's facilities in the "Canadian Pacific Rockies." "Yoho Valley Bungalow Camp," Peter Whyte, 1930, oil on canvas, 48.3 x 38.1 cm.

A Monarch of the Mountains
(Wapiti or Elk)

Looking down the Bow River Valley at Banff
Showing the re-constructed Banff Springs Hotel
The three pictures on this page are from paintings by Carl Rungius, N. A.

The Rocky Mountain Bighorn
(Mountain Sheep)

Carl Rungius, North America's foremost big game artist, frequently had his pieces used in Canadian Pacific advertising brochures after their format was changed in the twenties to allow for reproductions of landscape paintings

"The Cave Of The Great Glacier, B.C." F. M. Bell-Smith, 1888, oil on canvas, 75 x 100 cm.

"Canyon Of The Illecillewaet, B.C." F. M. Bell-Smith, 1890, watercolour, 87.5 x 62.5 cm.

French language tourist brochures became standard in CPR advertising during the thirties

A light-hearted poster which helped to promote the very popular Summer Tours program

Elaborate Around the World tour advertising, soon after Canadian Pacific's agreement with P & O ensured the continuation of the service

PACIFIC COAST TOURS
THROUGH THE CANADIAN ROCKIES

"THE EMPRESS" VICTORIA

· VANCOUVER · VICTORIA ·
BELLINGHAM · NEW WESTMINSTER
· SEATTLE · TACOMA ·
· PORTLAND · LOS ANGELES ·
· SAN FRANCISCO ·
CANADIAN PACIFIC RY.
1911

PACIFIC COAST TOURS
THROUGH THE CANADIAN ROCKIES

MT. STEPHEN, CANADIAN ROCKIES

· VANCOUVER · VICTORIA ·
BELLINGHAM · NEW WESTMINSTER
· SEATTLE · TACOMA ·
· PORTLAND · LOS ANGELES ·
· SAN FRANCISCO ·
CANADIAN PACIFIC RY.
1911

Victoria's new Empress Hotel vied with the Canadian Rockies as the feature for this 1911 Pacific Coast Tours brochure

133

A tastefully designed poster advertising the thrice daily service available between Toronto and Chicago in 1893 during the World's Fair

This colourful butterfly provided the cover for a butterfly-shaped leaflet advertising the Chicago World's Fair in 1893

A stylish brochure aimed at promoting the Chateau Frontenac and the tourist attractions of Quebec City

A page from CPR brochure, advertising the *Empress Steamship Lines*

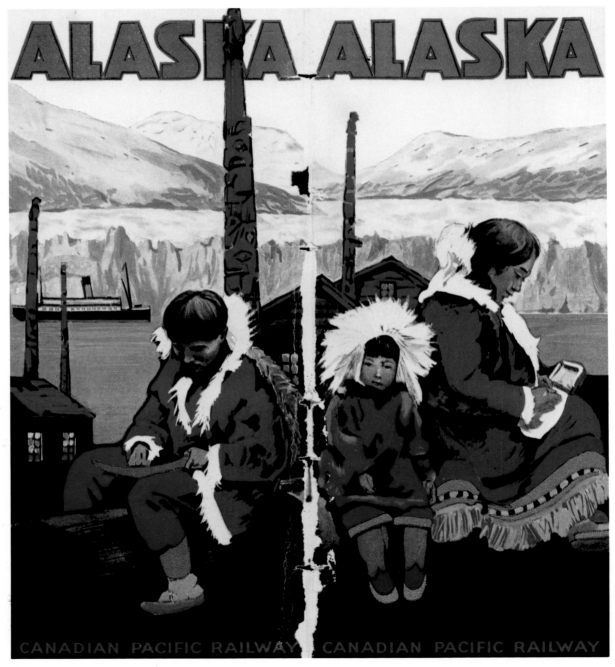

Realizing the desire of Americans to visit Alaska, tours via Canada quickly became a part of the company's promotional repertoire

Promotion of service to the Orient was still as much a concern to the company in the thirties as it had been at the time of its initiation in 1891

Perhaps the ultimate in CPR slogans was utilized to adorn the cover of this cruise brochure

Some of the most exotic and colourful commercial artwork ever produced was done for Canadian Pacific's cruise campaign in the twenties

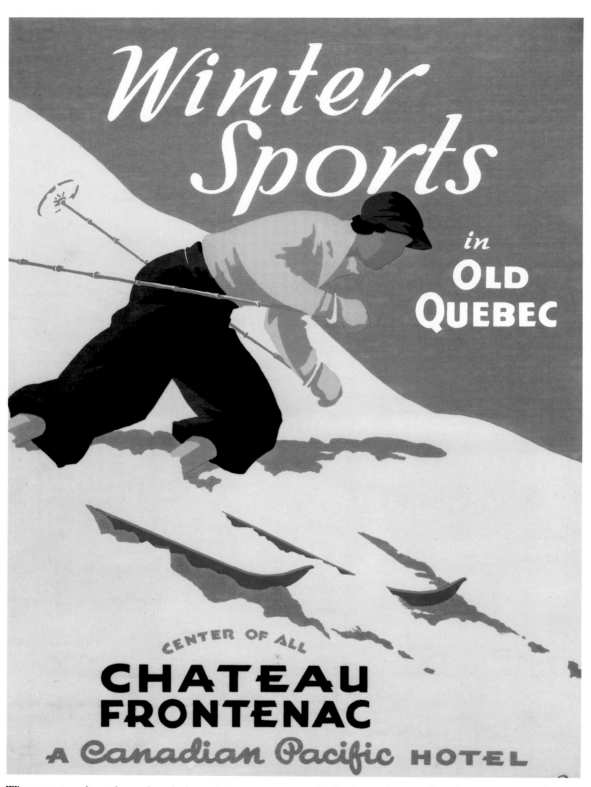

Winter sports such as tobogganing, skating and skiing were promoted in Quebec as a means of boosting off-season use of eastern lines and hotels

John Murray Gibbon's Sky Line Trail Hikers became a popular sister organization to the Trail Riders after its establishment in 1933

The Highland Gathering and Scottish Music Festival joined the older Banff Indian Days in the late twenties as special events to focus tourist attention on the CPR's mountain resort

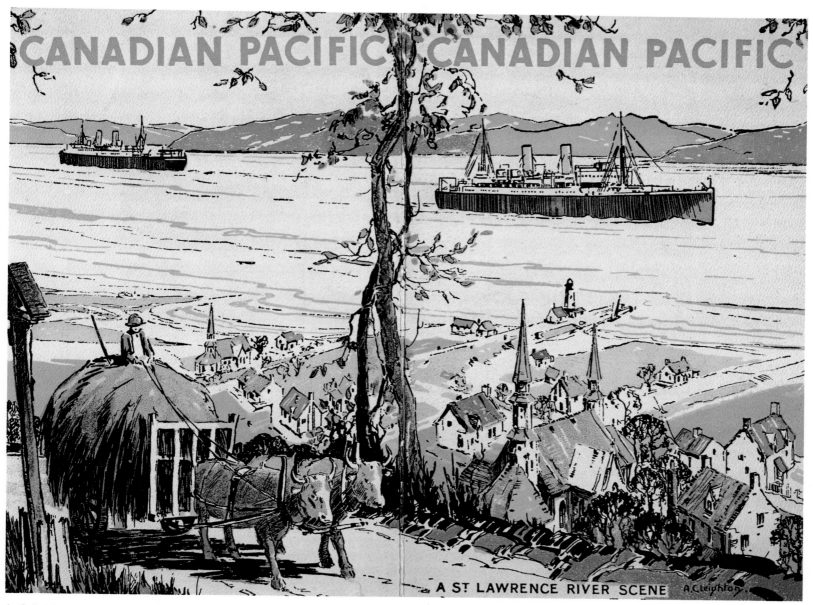

A ST LAWRENCE RIVER SCENE   A.C.Leighton.

A. C. Leighton, one of the company's most gifted artists and later one of western Canada's foremost landscape painters, produced numerous illustrations for brochures and posters in the last half of the twenties

RESORTS IN THE ROCKIES

CANADIAN PACIFIC

A popular Canadian cliché, the Mountie, was frequently used for tourist advertising in conjunction with the Canadian Rockies, by the twenties a cliché in themselves

R. H. Palenske, a Chicago artist, was one of those most frequently employed to illustrate promotional materials, such as this brochure cover for the Banff Springs Hotel in 1929

This booklet shows that the company was still as eager to promote British tourism to Canada in 1930 as it had been over forty years earlier with the issue of
The New Highway to the East

A thirties poster promoting one of the major attractions of Canadian Pacific's Algonquin Hotel at St. Andrews by the Sea in New Brunswick – its world class golf course

A 1930 advertising brochure for the second *Empress of Japan*, illustrated on the following four pages, demonstrated the height of quality and good taste in tourist advertising material

PRESENTING

The New

EMPRESS OF JAPAN

fastest to the Orient

First Class Dining Room

Bed Room of a de Luxe Suite

Sitting Room of a de Luxe Suite

Advertising for Canadian Pacific cruises continued all through the depression, this poster dating from the early thirties

Other company steamship services were not neglected despite strong promotion of the cruise program, as shown in this late twenties poster advertising its *Duchess* service

The
ROYAL YORK
TORONTO · CANADA

LARGEST HOTEL in the BRITISH EMPIRE

Canadian Pacific's new Royal York Hotel in Toronto, advertised as the largest in the Commonwealth, was opened with much fanfare in 1929

Motorized transportation became an important part of Canadian Pacific's tourist services in the mountains during the twenties. Byron Harmon photograph

The CPR recognized the need to support the creation of national parks in order to preserve the magnificent scenery in the neighborhood of Glacier House and its other mountain hotels. Notman photograph

With the provision of outfitting and guiding services at Banff, exploration of the mountains quickly extended south to Mount Assiniboine, promoted in the "Swiss" campaign as "the Matterhorn of the Canadian Rockies." Vaux family photograph

The Vaux family's glacial pursuits, which were assisted by the CPR, are graphically illustrated in this view of George Vaux taken in 1898 at the toe of the Illecillewaet Glacier next to the mark "Edge of ice VII-16-1887." Vaux family photograph

The CPR-sponsored Banff Indian Days, which featured a daily parade of natives in full regalia, provided a shot in the arm for the fledgling economy of the tourist town. Elliott Barnes photograph

Company assistance to climbers and tourist-explorers extended to free transportation on freight trains and the loan of railway speeders. Vaux family photograph

The CPR's first canvas-rooved cabins on the shore of Emerald Lake, the forerunner of Emerald Lake Chalet. Vaux family photograph

The CPR's Swiss guides were pleased when they could find tourists willing to venture beyond the foot of the Illecillewaet Glacier. Vaux family photograph

The acquisition of the Algonquin Hotel at St. Andrews by the Sea in 1905 marked the first significant move by Canadian Pacific into Maritimes tourism

The construction of the Chateau Frontenac and Place Viger Hotels in Quebec in the nineties was followed by a concerted advertising campaign to make the province a popular tourist destination

The CPR's 1891 brochure advertising its first round-the-world tours on the new *Empresses*

A pusher locomotive on one of the Big Hill's three escape tracks near Field, B.C., 1885. O. B. Buell photograph

The recently completed Banff Springs Hotel in its magnificent setting with Van Horne's pavilion jutting out towards the Bow River.
Vaux family photograph

A joyous crowd turned out to meet the first train to arrive at the new terminus of Vancouver on May 23, 1887

The Pacific Express stands at Glacier station with Glacier House in the background in this view by William McFarlane Notman.
Movement of trains in this location often caused a stampede from the dining room, much to Van Horne's chagrin.
William McFarlane Notman photograph

George Ham (front center), "Ambassador-at-Large for the CPR," poses with members of the Canadian Women's Press Club at Calgary, 1913

Christmas card to Colonel George Ham from newspaper friends, 1924

Banff Springs Canadian National Park, which appeared in the early nineties, was the first company pamphlet devoted specifically to the mountains

Kate Reed's effective use of furniture and antiques is apparent in the furnishing of this Banff Springs Hotel suite. Byron Harmon photograph

Interior of the enlarged Mount Stephen House, 1902. Vaux family photograph

Beginning in the late twenties the CPR began to offer ski excursions as a way of extending the tourist season. Here skiers enjoy the slopes at Skoki, north of Lake Louise, in 1932. Byron Harmon photograph

Epilogue

There were two developments in CPR promotion in the late twenties and early thirties that deserve mention as significant factors in the company's future. One was the creation of special fares to counter passenger losses to the automobile and the other was an attempt to spread out the season for tourist traffic.

In its booklet *Canadian Pacific Facts and Figures*, which appeared in 1937, the company, for the first time, admitted that automobile tourism had hurt its business:

Within the past few years, and particularly the last decade, there has been a decided change in the sources from which emanate the movement of passengers by rail, due to the advent and development of new modes of transportation, chiefly that of the private automobile. While, at one time, the short haul local traffic constituted a considerable volume it is now much diminished, as reflected in such events as the Canadian National Exhibition, at Toronto. The movement by rail to this annual gathering of people from far and near was one calling upon the entire available passenger equipment. Now, although the attendance at the Big Fair has greatly multiplied, the rail passenger traffic has not followed the increase.

The company responded with a class of fare called the "bargain excursion" wherein greatly reduced ticket prices were offered to those travelling on short hauls at specified times, particularly on weekends when traffic was light. Eventually the plan included "bargain excursions" at non-peak times for trains travelling right across the country. For mountain visitors there was an "All Expense Tour of the Canadian Rockies," featuring one ticket at a fixed price covering return rail fare plus such expenses as transport, sightseeing, hotel accommodation and meals for a detour trip between Banff and Field. All-expense-paid tours caught on and soon became one of the most popular forms of tourist travel in Canada.

In its attempt to expand the tourist season the company turned to promotion of winter activities. Skating, curling, tobogganing and snowshoeing had been popular in eastern Canada from the earliest days of CPR service but it was not until after the building of company hotels that these old winter sports and a new one, skiing, were promoted to increase tourist traffic. Early interest in skiing centred on the Montreal area and after the formation of the Montreal Ski Club in 1904 club members began to take the occasional trip to the nearby Laurentians. In 1927 the CPR decided to run special trains from Montreal to the Laurentians as one-day ski excursions. The first decade of ski excursions yielded an elevenfold increase in passenger traffic and by the mid-thirties American skiers from New York and New England joined the Canadians on the Laurentian ski trains.

In the Canadian Rockies winter tourist promotion began in 1917 with the first Banff Winter Carnival. The Carnival became a stop on the North American ski-jumping circuit and attracted some winter visitors, but it was not until the thirties, with the development of skiing at Mount Norquay and at Skoki north of Lake Louise, that there was any significant winter tourist traffic. The choice of Banff as the site for the 1937 Dominion Ski Championships caused the CPR to dispatch the first Snow Trains to the resort. Eventually the development of skiing in the Banff area would lead to the opening of its major mountain hotels, the Banff Springs and the Chateau Lake Louise, during the winter months.

The company added the technical wonders of the age — motion pictures in the twenties and radio in the thirties — to its arsenal of tourist promotion weapons and the command posts multiplied to administer the all-embracing promotion program. By the mid-thirties the General Publicity Department headed by Gibbon consisted of four sections: Advertising, Press Bureau, Photograph Department and Art Department. Advertising took care of placing newspaper and magazine advertising as well as the preparation of advertising pamphlets and brochures and the selection and distribution of motion pictures. Of the 111 pamphlets it produced in 1936, 44 were for the Passenger Traffic Department, 42 for Canadian Pacific Steamships, and 25 for the Hotel Department. The Press Bureau, with branch offices at Winnipeg, Toronto, Vancouver, New York and London, supplied information and news of company activities and services to newspapers, magazines and other publications throughout the world. The Photograph Department supplied from its thousands of negatives on file

Byron Harmon captures Mount Stephen on his movie camera from Burgess Pass. The CPR began to use movie footage for tourist promotion widely in the twenties. Byron Harmon photograph

material for articles, books and the company's own promotional productions, as well as making available sets of lantern slides on various Canadian subjects. The Art Department prepared the layouts for pamphlets and designed posters, maps and menus as well as sharing in the responsibility for preparing CPR exhibits. Altogether the General Publicity Department was responsible for the preparation and distribution of more than 1,500,000 copies annually of Canadian Pacific publications dealing with tourist services, facilities and opportunities in the country.

The federal Department of Trade and Commerce estimated by the mid-thirties, not a particularly good time for tourism, that the annual value of "Canada's greatest invisible export"

was $260,000,000. The CPR was still a significant force in generating tourist traffic but by this time the government of Canada and Canadian National Railways had also become major tourist promoters, to be joined by provincial governments as they recognized the importance of tourism to their economies. But undeniably the CPR had laid the groundwork for Canadian tourist promotion. For a period of fifteen years after the completion of its transcontinental line it had been virtually the only agency promoting tourism in Canada and from the turn of the century until the First World War it received only marginal assistance from the government and other railways. As Van Horne had hoped, the CPR put Canada on a highway and made it better known to both the world and itself.

A Note on Sources

Because of the nature of this work, I did not feel it was necessary to cite specific sources. In most cases, the source of quoted material is obvious from the text. However, I feel it would be useful to say a few general things about the interesting material available on the subject of the CPR and Canadian tourism.

As far as original material is concerned, this manuscript was heavily dependent on four sources. The first was Van Horne's correspondence files, available in the form of outgoing letterbooks and, to a lesser degree, incoming correspondence files at the CPR Corporate Archives in Montreal (the letterbooks are also available in microform through the Public Archives of Canada). The second major source was the extensive amount of promotional material, referred to in the text, issued by the CPR over the years. Many archives and libraries in Canada have collections of such material but those I found most useful were at the CPR Corporate Archives, the Glenbow Archives, the Archives of the Canadian Rockies and the British Columbia Provincial Archives. A third source was the accounts of the tourists themselves, particularly in the period up to the turn of the century. These are extensive and, again, are available in numerous historical libraries across the country. Finally, the best original source of material for the final part of the story was John Murray Gibbon's unpublished autobiography entitled "Scot to Canadian — One of More than a Million," written in 1951. A copy of this is available at the Archives of the Canadian Rockies.

Secondary sources vary from the general to the specific. Three general reference books on the CPR which I found particularly useful were Omer Lavallée's *Van Horne's Road*, W. Kaye Lamb's *History of the Canadian Pacific Railway* and Harold Innis' *A History of the Canadian Pacific Railway*. On specific aspects of tourism there were also some important secondary sources to be consulted. On the subject of the history of tourism I found that very little had been written; however, one source which did prove valuable was Edmund Swinglehurst's *The Romantic Journey*, which provides an excellent picture of the British background. An indispensable source on the topic of CPR immigration promotion is J.B. Hedges'

Building the Canadian West. For a very complete and accurate background on CPR artists, at least the first wave, Dennis Reid's landmark book *Our Own Country Canada* was consulted. Information on the CPR's involvement with steamships was found in George Musk's *Canadian Pacific, The Story of the Famous Shipping Line*. Three books on CPR hotels that were found useful were Harold Kalman's *The Railway Hotels and the Development of the Chateau Style in Canada*, Bart Robinson's *Banff Springs, The Story of a Hotel* and William Putnam's *The Great Glacier and its House*. Works on or by the main protagonists in the story are also important, including Walter Vaughan's *The Life and Work of Sir William Van Horne*, George Ham's *Reminiscences of a Raconteur* and John Murray Gibbon's *Steel of Empire*. Material on the CPR's relationships with the federal government vis-a-vis national parks is available in several collections at the Archives of the Canadian Rockies and in the annual commissioner's and superintendent's reports that formed part of the Department of the Interior *Reports*. For information on the CPR's relationship with its concessionaires in the mountains, my own two books, *Diamond Hitch, The Early Outfitters and Guides of Banff and Jasper* and *The Brewster Story* should be consulted. And finally, a little handbook that is vital for any aspect of CPR history is *Canadian Pacific Facts and Figures*, published in 1937.

Sources of visual material are also legion, but the reader may find information on these in the photographic credits.

O. B. Buell's "The Chancellor near Leanchoil," part of a portfolio presented to Van Horne in 1885, was lent to John Fraser as a reference for a sketch which, in the form of an engraving, was used in CPR promotional material. O. B. Buell photograph

Index

Illustration credits

Canadian Pacific Corporate Archives: 6, 9, 13, 14, 17, 22, 23, 25 (bottom right), 27, 29, 33, 34, 35, 43, 44, 48 (left), 52, 62, 70, 72, 73, 76 (left), 79, 80, 83 (left), 84 (left), 86 (top), 93, 96, 98, 105, 109, 122 (left & right), 131, 132 (left & right), 134, 135, 136, 138, 139, 142, 143, 144 (left), 146, 147, 148, 149, 154, 155, 156, 164 (left & right), 165, 170 (right), 171, 177, 178 (bottom), back cover

City of Vancouver Archives: 22 (top left)

Glenbow Museum: front cover, 10 (bottom right), 16, 26, 28, 31, 38, 39, 40, 42, 69, 74 (left), 76 (right), 83 (right), 110-111, 112 (bottom), 116 (left & right), 120, 123, 126 (right), 127, 166 (inset), 170 (left)

Grace, Dr. Donald: 126 (left), 130 (left & right)

Lavallée, Omer: 4, 19, 53, 112 (top), 166, 178 (top)

National Gallery of Canada: 115, 124, 125

Notman Photographic Archives: 30, 32, 113, 114, 117, 118 (left), 158

Peter and Catharine Whyte Foundation:
Archives of the Canadian Rockies: 10 (centre, bottom left & top right), 12, 24, 25 (top left), 45, 46, 47 (left & right), 48 (right), 49, 50, 51, 56 (left & right), 57, 58, 59, 60, 61, 63, 64, 65, 66, 67, 71, 77, 78, 82, 84 (right), 88, 89, 90, 91, 92 (left & right), 94, 95, 99, 100, 102, 104, 106, 107, 108, 119, 121, 129, 133, 137, 140, 141, 144 (right), 145, 150-53, 157, 159, 160 (left & right), 161, 162, 163, 167, 169, 172, 173, 174, 176
Peter Whyte Gallery: 1, 37, 54, 128

Provincial Archives of Alberta (Ernest Brown Collection): 10 (top left), 75 (left & right), 118 (right)

Provincial Archives of British Columbia: 18, 20, 168

Provincial Archives of Manitoba: 86 (bottom), 87

Public Archives of Canada: 15

Vancouver Maritime Museum: 68, 74 (right), 85

Design: Scott Thornley, STDA
Art Production: Bruce Aitken, STDA
Production Assistance: Susan Sopoci, Margaret Deveaux, Lianne Ritchie, STDA
Typesetting: Headlines, Word for Word
   Text: Crocker Bryant Inc.
Printing: Dai Nippon